AN

ENGLISH AND HINDOOSTANEE

NAVAL DICTIONARY

OF

TECHNICAL TERMS AND SEA PHRASES

AN

ENGLISH AND HINDOOSTANEE

NAVAL DICTIONARY

OF

TECHNICAL TERMS AND SEA PHRASES,

SHORT GRAMMAR

BY LIEUTENANT THOMAS ROEBUCK

GYAN

Published by

GYAN

Gyan Publishing House
5, Ansari Road
Daryaganj, New Delhi-110002
Phone: 011-47034999, 9811692060
E-mail: books@gyanbooks.com

Distribution Network
gyanbooks.com
India, USA, Canada, UK, Australia

ISBN: 978-81-212-5973-6 (PB)
First Published, 1813

2nd Impression 2024

Printed at: Gyan Press, Delhi.

AN ENGLISH AND HINDOOSTANEE NAVAL DICTIONARY OF TECHNICAL TERMS AND SEA PHRASES
Author: LIEUTENANT THOMAS ROEBUCK

AN

ENGLISH AND HINDOOSTANEE

NAVAL DICTIONARY

OF

TECHNICAL TERMS AND SEA PHRASES,

AS ALSO

THE VARIOUS WORDS OF COMMAND GIVEN IN WORKING A SHIP, &c.

WITH MANY SENTENCES OF GREAT USE AT SEA;

THE WHOLE

Calculated to enable the Officers of the Hon. East-India Company's and Country Service to give their orders to the Lascars with that Exactness and Promptitude which, upon many Occasions, must prove of the greatest Importance.

BY THE LATE

CAPTAIN THOMAS ROEBUCK.

OF THE MADRAS ESTABLISHMENT, ACTING EXAMINER AND ASSISTANT SECRETARY IN THE COLLEGE OF FORT-WILLIAM.

FOURTH EDITION.

REVISED AND CORRECTED BY

WILLIAM CARMICHAEL SMYTH ESQ.

LATE OF THE HON. EAST INDIA COMPANY'S BENGAL CIVIL SERVICE.

1848.

EXTRACT

FROM

THE PREFACE

OF

CAPTAIN THOMAS ROEBUCK.

It is with the utmost diffidence that I presume to lay the following Sheets before the Public: but I trust that the general utility of a work of the kind, if properly executed, is a sufficient apology for the present attempt; especially when it is considered, that although we have many Native Seamen in our shipping, there is no work to be had, which is calculated to enable an Officer of a ship to give his orders, or carry on a conversation with the Lascars, upon the most common occurrences connected with his several duties.

To obviate this, I have not only translated all the words and phrases I could find in several English Naval works, but also availed myself of the leisure afforded by a long passage between England and India, in collecting all the words of command, &c. which I heard made use of in the actual working of the ship, as well as by consulting Captain THOMAS DUMBLETON, and the officers of the Honorable Company's extra ship Larkins, whenever I was at a loss with respect to the exact meaning of any English sea term; and I must here acknowledge how much I owe to their kindness on many occasions. The very satisfactory manner in which they explained every difficulty, which in the course of my *nautical studies*, I had occasion to trouble them with, demands my most sincere thanks.

The work from which I have received the greatest assistance is entitled "The Midshipman's, or British Mariner's Vocabulary, being an Universal Dictionary of Technical Terms and Sea Phrases, used in the Construction, Equipment, Management, and Military Operations of a Ship. By J. J. MORE. Second Edition. London, 1805." This invaluable work may be considered as the ground work of the English part of my Dictionary, which my kind friend, Captain DUMBLETON, was so obliging as to read over, and to insert in it such useful terms as had inadvertently been omitted, and, at the same time, to mark those words which appeared to him to be of little or no use in a Hindoostanee Naval Dictionary. This will account for many words having been left out, either from their being more applicable to the Royal Navy, to European navigation, or to that advanced state of nautical science, which distinguishes the nations of Europe from those of Asia.

It is necessary to mention, in this place, that an immense number of English, Portuguese, and other words are used by the Lascars, but, often so completely changed by them in pronunciation, that it is difficult to say whether they be corruptions or not. As the greater number of the corruptions are English words, I have denoted them in the Italic character, as corresponding with that in which the English portion of the Dictionary is printed; but, upon the grand plea of utility, I have thought it advisable to retain the words in their corrupted state, as being, in my opinion, better understood by the Lascars. Such words must, however, be pronounced agreeably to the powers of the letters, as exhibited in pages 1 and 2.

All words corrupted from the Portuguese and other languages are printed in Roman type, and I have generally mentioned at the bottom of the page to what language they belong; however, this is more a matter of curiosity than of utility. The attentive reader will quickly perceive, that a considerable portion of the words used by the Lascars are corruptions of Portuguese, which may be accounted for, in a great measure, from their having been the first navigators in this part of the globe.

In consequence of not being able to obtain appropriate Hindoostanee terms for some few English words, I first intended to have left them out; but, upon the consideration that some persons might hereafter be more fortunate, I inserted them in their proper places.

I wrote all the words as pronounced to me, at the time, by ULEE* *Surhung* of the Larkins, and after my arrival here *overhauled* his pronunciation, in his own presence, by the assistance of SHEKH DUOLUT *Surhung*, from Islamabad *or* Chu*t*ga*n*w,** SHEKH MOOHUMMUD *Surhung*,

* A native of Kuch,h. I found him a most intelligent man; and it is but just to mention, that I received the greatest assistance from him in this work, as I found him not only extremely willing and active, but also particularly well-qualified for the task, having been employed about twenty years in the Country Service of Bombay and this Port, by which means he was enabled to furnish me with such words as are generally used by the Lascars of both places.

** Vulgarly, Chittagong.

from Koolabu,* and Yoosoof *Surhung*, from G,hog,ha; however, it must be allowed, that even they differ considerably in their pronunciation of many words throughout the work, as might be expected, considering that they all four come from parts of India widely distant from each other; I have therefore made it my study, not only to obtain the various modes of pronuncing the same word, but also to get those terms made use of by the Lascars from different Sea-Ports of India, and I have generally mentioned, in the form of a note, by whom the particular word is used, so as to enable an Officer of a Ship to adapt his language to whatever set of Lascars he may happen to have under his command.

To every person who is qualified to make the experiment, upon trial it will at once appear evident, that there is little difference between the rules of the high or Court Hindoostanee, and the dialect spoken by the Lascars; at least, in my opinion, the distinction is not so great as between the polished language of our own country, and that spoken by the seamen on board of English ships. The fact is this, that the distinction be-

---

* The Coilabby mentioned in Orme's History o India.

tween the high Hindoostanee, and that jargon as spoken by the Lascars, consists in a number of words from the English, Portuguese, and other languages, being introduced into the latter, and not in the application of the rules. Independant of this, many Hindoostanee words are used by the Lascars, which are perfectly unintelligible to the natives ashore, as is the case in our own language.

To those who have not leisure or inclination to study the First Principles of this language, so as from the body of the Dictionary, to form such sentences, or give such orders as they may wish to the Lascars, the Words of Command and Sea Phrases, at the end of the book, will be found particularly convenient. I must here acquaint the Reader, that it has been more my endeavour to express the English sentences in the language and idiom of the Lascars, than to give a literal translation of them, which would not be so well understood.

A

NAVAL DICTIONARY,

ENGLISH AND HINDOOSTANEE.

Aback, Baksee.

Abaft, Peechˌhil.

Abaft the beam, Brandul ke peechˌhe.

To abandon (leave), Chˌhor jana, *or* dena.

Able bodied, Bˌhula bˌhaˌee.

Aboard (a boat), Bot pur, muchwe pur, *(a ship),* Juhaz pur (*or* men), *i. e. in the ship.*

To go aboard, Juhaz pur jana.

To fall aboard of, Ara purna, juhaz pur jakur girna.

To go about, Pˌherkur jana.

About, Pˌher, pˌherke, gˌhoomke.

Abreast, Luge-luge, burabur.

Abroad, Pur-des, sufur koon *or* ko.

Absent, Ghuer hazir, hazir nuˌee.

Aburton, Ara.

Accommodation ladder or chair, Seerˌhee, seeree, koorsee, chuokee.

Acorn, Topee.

Action, Luraˌee.

Admiral, Atmural.

Adrift, Ch,hoo*t*a, mara mara.

Advice boat, Khubur ka muchwa.

Adze, Busoola, vansla.

Afloat, Bhunsta, tira.

Afore, Agil, agul.

Aft, Peech,hil, p,hich,-hwara. *Right*, Jàhom, yahom.

After, Peech,hil ka.

After guard of a watch, Peech,hil wâle, pee-ch,hil ka poree.

After sail, Peech,hil ka ser,h *or* sur.

Aground, Ch,hee*t*a, luga, sook,he pur chu*r*ha, u*r*a, u*t*ka.

Ahead, Agil, agul.

Aim, Shust, du*t*, tak.

To air, Huwa k,hilana, huwa me*n* dena.

Alee, Boordoo.

All, Sub, tumam, sara.

Allowance, Resum, *perhaps from ration, (full)*, Poora resum, *(short)*, Kum resum.

To stop allowance, Resum bund kurna.

Aloff, Door, tufawoot.

Aloft, Oopur, dol pur.

Along side, Boordoo me*n*, b,hi*r*ke.

Along shore, Kinare kinare.

Lying along shore, Kurwu*t* hoke.

Amain, Sub milke, ek dum, ek,hee zor se

Amidships, Beech-a-beech, beech me*n*.

Ammin for the lead, Proom kee churbee, gul gul. *See lead.*

Ammunition, Baroot-golee.

Anchor, Nungur, lungur.

Anchor, shank, Nungur

kee *d*un*d*ee, ka*n*ree, *or* kandee. *Eye*, Nungur ke anile ka ch,hed. *Ring*, Nungur ka anila. *Nut*, Nungur ka 'kan. *Palms of*, Lungur ke dant ka soop*r*a. *Crown*, Nungur ka go*n*r. *Stock*, Nungur ka danga. *Bill*, Nungur ke soop*r*e kee nok. *Flukes of*, Koondee. *Arms of*, Lungur ka dant.

Sheet anchor, *Sheet* nungur, akbutee lungur. *This last term is much used by the Bengal lascars.*

Best bower anchor, Bura nungur.

Small bower anchor, Ch,ho*t*a nungur, chaloo nungur.

Anchor kedge, *Kej* nungur, lohe ka dange wala.

Anchor stream, *Lot,*-haree nungur.

To cast anchor, Lungur *d*alna, *or* ch,ho*r* dena.

To weigh anchor, Lungur *oot*hana.

At anchor, Lungur pur, nungur baree.

Anchorage, Lungur kurne ka *or* (kee) juguh.

An end, K,hu*r*a.

Angle, Kona.

To answer, Juwab dena, chulna, bunna, hona. *The helm*, Manna.

Apeck, *Peek*, sa*t*.

Apron, Runjuk ka seesa *or* d,hukna.

Arms, Hut,hiyar.

Ashore, Kinare. *(Aground)*, Kinare pur.

Astern, Peech,hil.

At, pur.

Athwart, A*r*a ben*d*a.

Athwart hawse, Samne ara pura.

Avast, Bus, bus bus, ruho ruho, han han.

A weather, *See Weather*.

A weigh, Utrung. *See anchor a trip*.

Awning, Ch,hutree.

B.

To back the sails astern, *Baksee* kurna agil peech,hil.

Back board, Peet,hka tukthu.

Backler, Ank,h ka chupul, *or* p,honta.

Back stay, Pet furodee.

After back stay, Peech,-hil furodee, *or* peech,-hil brandul. (*)

To bag pipe the mizen, *Boom* luptee uriya kurna.

To balance a sail, Goomee band,hna.

To bale, Panee nikalna.

Ballast, Neerum, neelum, leelum.

Bank or shoal, Chur, khurabu.

Bare Poles, *See Poles*.

Barge, B,hur.

Barnacle, Kaloo, lona keera.

Bay, Goob, goop.

Beach, Kinaru.

Beacon, Buota, vuota katee.

Beam, *Beem*, ara.

To bear in with the land, Kinare kinare jana (*or* ana).

To bear down upon, Sor purna.

To bear off, Dufrana.

To be becalmed, Huwa bund hona.

(*) This comes from the Portuguese word *brandaes*, back stays.

Bed, Kooniyan.

Before, Agil, agul.

To belay, Band,hna.

Belaying pin, Tolut, toolut.

Bell, G,huree.

To bend, Giruh marna.

To bend the cable, Maliya band,hna.

Bends, Kumur-bund.

Bentick shrouds, Faltoo arvil.

Between decks, Tootuk ke beech.

Bight, Goobba.

Bill boards,

Bilboes, Beree ka seekh.

To bilge, Tootna, torna.

Bilge-water, Gamut ka panee, boomba ka panee.

Binnacles, *Koompas* ka g,hur.

Binnacle lamps, *Koompas* ka fanoos.

Birth, Juguh, mukan.

To bit the cable, *Habeet* men humar dalna.

Bitts, *Habeet*, *abit*. (*)

Bitt stopper, *Habeet* ka bosu.

Block, Kupee.

Blocksheave, Kupee ka roda. (**)

Block pin, Kupee kee chabee. (***)

Aboard, Manch, gos *is used by the Bengal lascars*.

Board and board, Manch uor manch.

Boarding netting, *Boordoo* kee jalee.

Boarding pike, B,hala, burch,hee.

Boat, Muchwa.

(*) *Port*, Abitas. (**) *Port*, Roda.
(***) *Port*, Chave.

Long boat, Lang bot.

Boat hook, Bot hook.

Boatswain, Bosman, bochman; if a native, surhung.

Boatswain's mate, Bosman ka *met,* bura *t*un*d*el.

Bobstay, Bawustue, ool*t*a suwa,ee. *This last is used often, in asking a raw lascar, where the bobstay is, by way of joke.*

Bold shore, Saf kinaru, kinare nuzdeck kunal.

Bolt, Kubeelu, kuveelu.

Bolt rope, Het,hee kee alat.

Bonnet.

Boom, Boom.

Bore (of a gun), Gol moorree.

Bore or boar in the river Ganges, Hoomma, hoomba, ban, sur.

Bottom (that part of the ship in the water), Pee*t*,h. *Of the sea,* Tuliya.

Bound, Bund. *Gammoning;* Bo,ee bund.

Bow, Taliyamar ke pas.

Bowline, Boolin.

Bowline cringle, Boolin ka koo*n*iya*n*.

Bowsprit, Subdura.

Bowsprit cap, Subdura ka tok. *Shrouds,* Subdura lubran.

A brace, Bras.

To brace, Bras lugna, *or buras* lugna.

To brace sharp up, Bras chikar lugna.

Brail, Istingee.

To brail up, Istingee champna.

To break bulk, K,han k,holna.

Break water, Asra, pooshtu.

To break sheer, Gendra marna.

Breast fast, *Lasun* ka bosu.

Bridle, *Boolin* ka panw.

Brig, Do dolee juhaz.

To bring to, *See*, *to lie to*.

To bring up, Nungur *d*alna, *or* chˌhorna.

To broach to, *Baksee* ana, pˌher jana.

Broadside, Arabu,* suluk. *See Volley.*

Broken backed, Kumuree *too*t*ela juhaz.

Bucket, Baldee, baltee.*

Built, Bunela, bunaya.

Bulk heads, Tukhte ke deewal.

Bumkin, *Boomkin*.

Bumkin of a boat, Muchwe ka *boomkin*.

Bum boat, Dookan kee pˌhunsoˌee, *bambot*.

Bunt, Serˌh ka pe*t*.

Buntline, Bätlee.

Buoy, Boya, *boˌe*

Life buoy, Girela (*or* gira) admee buchane ka boˌe.

Burton, Burtun yaree.

Butt, Tukhte ka sandˌha *or* chandˌha *or* sandˌh.

Button (of a sail), Jee*t*, jˌhee*t*.

By the board, Tootuk ke burabur.

By the head, Sir bue*t*ˌhela, agil bˌharee.

By the wind, Baˌo ke moo*n*ˌh me*n*.

C

Cabin, Kamura, *from the Portuguese word camara, a cabin, etc.*

Cable, Humar.**

Sheet cable, *Sheet* ankur ka humar, akbutee

* *Port.* Balde.

** *Port.* Amarra.

humar.

Best bower cable, Bura humar.

Stream cable, Lot,haree humar.

To bitt the cable, Humar pur *habeet* band,hna.

Cable tier, Humar kee juguh, humar sungla kurne kee juguh.

Cablet, Ch,hota humar, *virndor*. *See Tow line*.

Call (boatswain's), Seetee.

Callipers, Map, *koopas or koompas*.

A calm, Kulmuriya, koormuriya, hulmuriya. (*)

To become calm, Koormuriya purna.

Camboose or caboose, Chooldan.

Can (jug), Lota, *pat* (*from pot*).

Canhooks, *Hook* wala *sling*.

Cannister shot, Kirich ka gola.

Cannon, Top.

To cannonade, Topan (*or* top) marna.

Cannon ball, Gola.

Canoe, Doonga, dengee.

To cant, D,hulkana, p,hirana.

Canvas, Wilayutee *tat*, ser,h ka kupra, nojir, *kanvees*.

Cap, Tok.

Cap for the head, Topee.

Cap (apron of a gun), Surposh.

Cape, Tek, tenk, *pont*, *sees*.

Cappanus, Durya ka keera, lona keera.

To capsize, *ooltana*,

* *Port*. Calmaria.

oohut dena, tul oopur kurna.

Capstern or capstan Duor, duowur. *In small vessels the capstan is called* cheena duor.

Capstan bar, Duor ka *baree.*

Capstan pall, Duor ka *pal.*

Captain (if an European), *Kuptan.*

(If a native of India, Arabia or Persia), Nakhooda.

(If from Sind, Kutch, Halar or Porbundur), Nakhwa, wanut *or* wannut.

To careen a ship, Juhaz ko wura kurna, *or* oorra kurna.

Cargo, B,hurtee, bar, boj,ha,ee.

Carlings, Kata baree.

Carpenter, Mistree, sootar, bur,hue. *Mate,* Mistree ka *met.*

Carriage, Top kee garee.

Carronade, Tooka top, tumboora top.

To carry away, Toot, jana, torna.

Cartel, Quedee puhoonchane ka juhaz.

Cartouch, Tosdan.

Cartridge, *Kartoos,* tota, *or* tonta. *Box in a ship,* *Kartoos* ka bakus.

Case shot, Ch,heenta gola.

To cast, Ph,enkna, dalna.

To cast (to fall off, as a ship), P,hirna.

To cast off, Ch,hor dena.

Cast away, Guya-goozra, tubah hoo,a. *See*

Wreck.

To be cast away, as a person, Tuwa,ee k,hana. *As a ship, Toot* jana, mara jana.

Catamaran, Kutmural, kutmuram, purancha, *properly a raft, which see. The man, Kutmural* wala.

Cat block, Ket kupa.

Cat fall, Ket ka *fal.*

Cat head, Ket.

Cat harpings, Ket arvil.

Cat hook, Ket hook.

Cat stopper, Ket ka bosu.

Cat-o-nine tails, Koordum, (*) *ket.*

Cat's paw, Goomta huwa.

To caulk, Kal puttee kurna.

Caulker, Kal puttee. (**)

Caulking, Kal puttee ka kam.

Caulking mallet, Moogra.

Caulking iron, Kal puttee ka batalee.

Ceiling, Ch,hutree.

Centre of a fleet, Fleet ka beech.

Centry or sentry, Suntree, pora-dar.

To chaff, G,husura lugna.

Chain, Zunjeer, sankul, (***) sankur.

Chain board, Mez *or* mej. (****)

Chain pump, Zunjeer ka bumba. (*****)

Chain plate, Mez ka loha *or* pu*tt*a.

(*) *Port.* Cordao. — (**) *Port.* Calafate. — (***) *Sunskrit.* Srink,hulu. — (****) *Port.* Mesa, *a board.* — (*****) *Port.* Bomba.

Chain shot, Zunjeeree gola.

Chain wales or channels, Mez, me*n*ch.

Chains, M*oo*tam ka pu*tt*a.

Channel, D,har.

Mid-channel, Munj d,har.

Charnel, Mej.

Chart, Nuqshu, pu*t*.

Chase, B,hagne wala, b,huggoo.

To chase, K,huderna, peech,ha kurna.

Chaser, Pich,h-luggoo.

Cheeks of the mast, T,hapa, dol ka kan.

To cheer, Sulamee ka hoorra kurna.

Cheerly, Khooshee se, juldee.

Chesstrees, Bu*r*e moore kee mankree.

Chest, Pe*t*ee, sundooq. *Arm*, Bundooq kee pe*t*ee. *Colour*, Nishan kee pe*t*ee, buota kee pe*t*ee.

To chinse, Ch,h*oo*ree se kal puttee kurna.

Chisel, Batalee, veenju*n*a.

Chock a block, Chikar.

Chocks of the rudder, S*oo*kan ka p,hanta.

To chop about, Huwa g,h*oo*mna.

Cistern, Tup.

Clamps of a gun carriage, Puttu. *Of a ship*,

To clap on, Lugana, bund kurna, puku*r* lena, band,hna.

To claw off, P,hirakur bar (bahur) jana.

Clear (*as water*), Saf, nirmul, khalee. (*Not cloudy*), P,hurch,ha, k,hoola.

Clear coast, Saf kinaru. *Hawse*, *See Hawse*.

To clear, Saf kurna.

To clear the land, Zumeen se nikul jana.

To clear the hold, K,hun se usbab nikalna.

To clear for action, Lurne ko tueyar kurna.

Cleat, Mankree, mukree.

Clinch, Maliya.

Clinched, Bund hoo,a.

Close haul'd, Chikar *bras, bras* chikar.

Close quarters, Boordoo b,her *or* b,heer.

Close weather, Kulmuriya. *See Calm.*

Clove hitch, See Hitch.

Clue, Koonyian.

Clue line, Istingee.

Clue garnet, Pulung. *See Clue.*

To clue up, Istingee kurna.

Coast, Kinaru.

Coaster, Kinare dek,hkur chulne wala.

Coasting on, Kinare pukurke jana.

Coat (jacket), Jaket. (In painting), T,hur, tuh, ponch.

Coboose, Chool lan.

Cockswain, Kaksen.

Coil (of a rope), Sankla.

Coir rope, Nariyul kee russee.

Collar of a stay, Suwa,ee ka goobba.

Colours, Vuota buota, nishan.

To come home, Chikar hona.

To come up with, Burabur ana *or* hona.

Commander, See Captain. (A mallet), Bura moogree *or* mongree.

Commodore, Kamador.

Companion, P,halke ka petee. (*Friend*), Dost, dostdar. (*Ladder*), Seer,hee.

Compass, Hookku, *koompas*.

Compliment, B,hurtee.

Conductor, Seekh.

Consort, Sat,h ka juhaz.

Continent, Bura kinaru, puta put muedan.

Convoy, Worawa, khuburdaree ka juhaz.

Cook, B,handaree, bawurchee.

Cooking place or galley, Chooldan, bawurchee-khanu.

Cooking kettle, Deg.

Coop (for fowls, &c.), Moorghee ka k,hupera.

Copper bottomed, Tambe p,haral *or* furar.

Cord, Musalee.

Cordage, Rusa-wusa, bund,hun-wundun.

Corposant.

Corpse, Moordu, lash.

A cot, K,hat jolee. (*For lascars*, &c.), Jolee. *See Hammock*.

Cove, K,hal, k,haree.

Counter, Duboosu.

Course Mojura.

Courses, (*)

Craft, B,hur. *See Lighter*, &c.

A crane, Kutree.

Crank, Oopur b,haree neeche khalee.

Creek, K,hol, k,hal. *See Cove*.

Creeper, Ch,hota grap-lin.

Crew, Juhazee, lushkur.

Crib (*for fowls*), Kupe-

(*) The *lascars* having no word for courses, it will be requisite to name all the sails included in this term.

ra. *See Coop.*

Cringle, Het,hee ka kooniyan.

Cross jack, Shak ser,h, shek sur.

Cross jack's yard, Shek-pirmun, *or* shek pur-wan.

Cross trees, Koorsee, danga.

Crow, *Kooro.*

Crowfoot, Mor panw. (*Lit.*) *the Peacock's foot.*

To crowd (*sail*), Ser,h t,hesum t,hes hukar-na.

Crown of an anchor, *See Anchor.*

Crowning, Ponte ka *p,hootin*, *or pootin.*

Cruise, K,hoorchun, sufeena.

To cruize, K,hoorchun kurna, sufeena p,hir-na.

A cruizer, K,hoorchun wala, sufeena wala.

Cuddy (*) (*in E. I. ships*), *Kuptan* k,ha-na k,hane kee juguh, (*literally, the Cap-tain's dining place* (*room*).

To cun, Chulana.

Cunning or conning, Sookanee kam.

Cunt line, *Peep* ka gala.

Current, Panee ka d,har, panee ka tor, panee ka wud.

To cut, Katna.

To cut and run, Humar kat ke b,hagna.

To cut off, Kat dalna.

Cutlass, Tulwar.

(*) I have not been able to get any term for cuddy; it is supposed to come from the *Persian* word *kudu*, a place, room, etc.

Cutter, Kutur, katur.

Cut water, Taliyamar. (*)

D.

Davit, Devee.

Day, Din, roz.

Dead body, Moordu, lash, mueyut. *Eye,* Mutam. *Lights,* Faltoo baree, p,haltoo baree. *Reckoning,* Tup ka shoomar. *Water,* Ghoomree k,hata panee G,hoomta panee. *Wood,* Put,han ka tagur.

To deaden a ship's way, Juhaz ko kum zor kurna, kum roos kurna, kum chaloo kurna.

Deck, Tootuk. (*Gun*) Beech ka tootuk. (*Main or wait*), Oopur ka beech ka tootuk. (*Orlop*), Neeche ka tootuk. (*Quarter*), Duor ke pas ka tootuk.

Deep sea-lead, Bura-proom. (**)

Deep sea-line, Bura proom kee alat *or* bura proom ka *luen.*

To depart, Ruwanu hona, nungur *oot,*hana.

Depth (*of water*), Oopur neeche, *oonda* panee.

To depress a gun, Neeche mojure ruk,hna.

Detachment, Jut,ha, gool.

Disabled (*as a lascar*), Lungra hoo,a. (*As a ship*), Loond boond.

To disband the lascars, &c., Ootar dena,

(*) *Port.* Talhamar.

(**) *Port.* Prumo.

ch,hor dena, bida kurna.

To discharge (*unload*), ootarna. (*A gun, &c.*), Ch,horna, marna, daghna.

Discipline (*regulation*), Bundobust. (*Punishment*), Suza, suja, mar peet.

To dismantle, Nunga kurna. Lunga kurna. (Nunga *signifies naked*).

Dismasted, Loond boond, nunga boonga. (*)

Dismounted, (*gun*), Gira hoo,a, *or* batil top.

To disobey an order, Hookm nu manna.

Division, Hissu, har.

Dock, Godee, *literally, the bosom.*)

Docking, Godee ke undur tanna.

Dock yards, Godee ka bunsar.

Dog, Lukree tanne ka *hook. Stopper*, P,haltoo (*or* faltoo) bosu. *Watch*, Ch,hota por.

Dolphin (*of the mast*), Juhaz ka *dalp,hin*.

Dolphin striker, Kawur.

Double-headed shot, Dandee *or* dundee wala gola.

To double a cape, Poonta (*or* tek) ch,hor dena.

To douse, *Suluk* kurna, nurum ruk,hna.

Down haul, *Ootara*.

Down haul tackles, *Duonhal* yaree.

Drag, Billee. (*In Hin-*

(*) *Perhaps from* nunga moonunga, *stark naked.*

doostanee billee *signifies a cat.*)

Drag rope, Pagur. (*A rope for dragging boats along the banks of the Ganges*), Goon. *Sticks* (*used on the banks of the Ganges*), B,huroo,a lukree, goon lukree.

To drag the anchor, Kusur (*or* kasur) kurna.

Draught, Panee, *as, of what draught is this ship?* yih juhaz kitna panee marta hue? Yih juhaz kitna panee torta hue? *is more used by the Bengal lascars than by those of Bombay, and Surat. See to draw.*

Draught (*of water, beer, &c.*), G,hoont.

To draw (*water as a ship*), Panee marna, (*or* mangna), panee torna. (*To pull*), Tanna, k,huenchna, le-jana.

To draw upon a ship, &c., Nuzdeek ana.

Drawing, Pukurna.

To dress a ship, Singarna.

Drift (*of the current*), Panee ka tan.

To drive, Ara jana, peech,he peech,he purna.

Driver, *Drawul.*

Driver boom, *Drawul boom.*

Driver boom top and lifts, *Boom* manteela, *boom* munteela, *or boom* manteel.

Drop, Chuora,ee. (*Of water, &c.*), Boond.

To drop anchor, Nungur dalna, lungur

kurna. *Astern*, Peech,he hu*t*na.

Duck (cloth), Doongree. (*The fowl*), Butuk, *wild duck*), Chukwa, chukwee.

Dunnage, Bich,hana, bich,hona *d*alun.

E.

Earrings, Mutwar.

To ease off or away (*a rope*), Nurm ruk,hna, t,hor*a* uriya kurna, tirkana.

East, Poorub, *oo*gmun, mushriq, mutl*u*.

To ebb, B,ha*t*,halugna *or* hona.

Eddy, B,huonree, g,hoomree, g,hoom*t*a panee.

To edge away, Kutrake jana *or* chula ana, tirch,ha chulna.

To elevate a gun, Top oopur mojure ruk,hna.

Embargo, G,ha*t* bund, bundun bund.

End (of a rope), Ponta.

An end, K,hu*r*a.

Engagement, Lu*r*a,ee.

Ensign, Nishan, buota, vuota.

To enter, or engage in service, Nuokuree qubool kurna, muheena lena.

To equip, Tueyar kurna.

Even keel, Erab burabur. *See Keel.*

Exercise, Quwa,*i*d.

Eye, Ank,h.

Eyes (*of a ship*), Juhaz kee ank,h.

Eye bolt, *Ue bol.*

Eyelet holes, Seekee ka ch,hed.

F.

Fag-end, Russee ka

ponta. (*) *See End.*

To fag out, K,hol jana.

Fair (as wind), Seed,ha, moowafiq, jahom, yahoom, yahom. (*Not cloudy*), P,hurch,ha, khoosh, saf, k,hoolasa. *See Clear.*

Fall, Fal.

To fall abroad, Ara purna, chur,h buet,-hna. (*Rather, to run down, q. v.*) *Astern,* Peech,he purna *or* ruhjana, peech,he hutna. *Calm,* Kurmuriya hona *or* purna, huwa gir jana. *See Calm.* *Down,* Gir purna. *Down the river,* Neeche jana. *Down (as a ship),* Bahur jana.

To fall in with, Milna, moolaqat kurna *or* hona.

Falling off, B,hare b,hare jana *or* purna.

False fire, or blue flames, Muhtab (*much used at sea by pilots and those in search of pilots*), morqm, moram.

Fashion pieces, Duboose ka *beem.*

To fasten, Muzboot kurna, bund kurna, band,hna.

Fathom, Wam, bam.

To fend off, Dufrana, talna.

Fenders, Dufra, dup,hra.

To fetch, Puhoonchna, jana, ponchna. *Away,* *Rol* k,hana, mara-mar p,hirna.

(*) *Port* Ponta.

Fid, Chabee, chavee.

Fiddle block, Gul ka*t*a kupee.

To fill, B,hurna, b,hurdena.

Fire, Ag.

To fire a gun, Ch,horua, marna, daghna. *See Gun.*

Firelock, Bundooq.

Fish, *See Anchor.*

Fish (*animal*), Much,hee, much,hlee.

(*For a mast, etc.*), Chupul, chapus; (*plural*) chupla*n*. *Fall*, *P,his fal*. *Gig*, Kawur, ka,or. *Hook*, Juhaz ka *p,his hook*. *Pendant*, *P,his* ka mat.

Fitting out, Tueyaree.

Flag, Nishan, wuo*t*a, ba,o*t*a.

Flag-staff (of a ship), Wuo*t*a katee, ch,hur ba*n*s.

Flat (*shallow*), Khurabu, chur.

Flaw, Goonj, huwa ka goonj.

Fleet, *P,hileet*, qafilu, b,har, buhr.

To fleet, Band,h ch,hor kurna, *p,hileet* kurna, mil ch,hor kurna.

Float, Purancha, trapa.

Float (*of a fishing line*), Turinda, tirinda, p,hutna, *used by the Bengal lascars.*

Floating, Id,hur ka ood,hur bu*n*sta p,hirta.

Flood, Juwar, b,hurtee. *See Tide.*

Floor, Juhaz ka pee*t*,h. *Timbers*, Kafinna, put,han ka *bank*.

The flow, Juwar, b,hurtee.

Flowing sheets, Ch,hoo*t*

damun, lurga *boolin.*

Flukes, See Anchor.

Flurry, P,hira huwa, *or* bet,ham huwa, g,hoomta huwa.

Flush fore and aft, Agil peech,hil saf.

To let fly the sheets, Damun ch,hor dena.

Foot (of a mast), Dol kee k,hampnee, dol kee paree, dol kee saree. *(Of a sail).* Neeche kee het,hee, neeche kee hent,hee. *Brails,* Neeche kee *istingee. Rope,* Neeche kee het,hee ka alad *or* alat. *Waleing,* K,hun ka furaree tukhtu.

To foot, Dufurana.

To forbid, Munu kurna.

To force over, T,hesum t,hes hukarna.

Fore, Agil, agul.

Fore and aft, Agil peech,hil. *Bow line,* Trikut *boolin. Braces,* Trikut *bras. Castle,* P,huna, (*) agul funa. *Castle men,* P,hune wale. *Catharpings,* Trikut ka *ket arveel. Hooks, See Breast hook. Jears,* Trikut pirmun ke *jer. Land,* Tek, tenk. *Lock,* P,hanta, kooniyan. *Mast,* Trikut dol. *Royal mast,* Trikut tubur dol, *or* trikut tubur koonda. *Runner, Marka.*

Fore sail, Trikut *or* tirkut. (**) *Shrouds,* Trikut lubran. *Stay,* Trikut suwa,ee. *Tac-*

(*) P,hun in Hindoostanee means the hood of a snake.

(**) *Port.* Traquete.

kle, Trikut suwa,ee yaree. *Top*, Trikut panjra. *See Top*. *Top gallant mast*. Trikut subur dol, trikut subur koonda. *Top mast*, Trikut gavee dol. *Top men*, Trikut panjre wale. *Tye*, Trikut *tu,ee* pur suwa,ee. *Yard*, Trikut pirmun, trikut purwan.

To fore reach upon, Agil bur,hna.

To form the line, Luen band,hna.

A former, Karboot, kalboot (*properly* kalbood).

Fort, Killa (*properly* qilu).

Forward, Agil, agul.

Foul, G,huree pura. *Anchor*, Umar ka nungur men bolta pura hue. *Bottom*, Peet,h pur kadee (*or* seepee). *Hawse*, Umar men bolta. *Rope*, G,huree puree alat. *Water*, Gudla panee, muela panee. *Wind*, Khurab huwa, khurab ba,o.

To run foul of, P,hunsana, P,hunsa jana.

To founder, Doob jana, mara jana, buet,h jana, ghurq hona.

Fox, *Paksee*.

Spanish fox, Sinjal.

Frapping, Kumur bund lena, lasun lena.

Frapping a ship, Juhaz ka kumur bund lena, lasun lena.

To go free, Damun jana, numta jana.

Freeing, K,hun ka panee sook,ha hurna.

Freight (*hire*), Nuol, noowul, kiraya.

Freight (cargo), Noowul ka mal.

Fresh (wind), T,hora zor huwa.

Fresh water, Meet,ha panee.

*Fresh water sailors** Meet,ha panee ke khulasee. *See Lubber.*

To freshen, Huwa uor b,hee t,hora hona.

To freshen hawse, Ank,h kee juguh men humar budulna.

Freshes, B,hat,he ka bura tan.

Frigate, *P,hriket*, *friket*.

Frigate built, *P,hriket* ka d,hup ka juhaz, juhaz ke oopur juesa *p,hriket* ka numoonu.

Full, B,hura.

Funnel. *P,hunel*.

To furl, Lupetna, qand,h lena.

Furling line, *G,haset*, *g,hanset*.

Fuse, Fuleetu, kakra.

Futtocks, Bank, wank.

Futtocks shrouds, *Putuk* sar, rikada.

G.

Gaff, Gosee pirmun, goosee purwan.

Gaff halliards, *Gu,ep,hul kunja*. *Top sail*, *Gu,ep,hul*.

Gage, *See Weathergage.*

To gain the wind, Wa,o pur jana.

Gale of wind, Toofan, and,hee. (*Hard or strong)*, Ulool toofan. *(Top gallant)* Subur k,holkur chulte toofan.

Galled, G,husora g,husura.

Gallery (quarter), Kun-

(*) It is singular that the lascars use the very same phrase that we do.

deel. *(Stern)*, Duboosu.

Galley, Chooldan.

Gallows bitts, Dewee.

Gammoning, Bo,e bund.

Gang, Jut,ha, tolee.

Gang board, Chal ka tukhtu.

Way, *Gangwue*.

To bring to the gangway, Suza dena, marna.

Garboard streak, Put,-han ka tagur.

Garland, Jale ka jolee.

Shot garland, Golee ka doonga.

Garnet, Bura suwa,e yaree.

Gasket, *G,hanseet*, *g,haset,h*.

Bunt, *gasket*, Pet *g,hanseet*.

To gather aft a sheet, Damun chikar kurna.

To gather away, Roos ziyadu hona, guon se chulna.

Gears, *See Jears*.

Gimbals,*Koopas* ka puta.

Gimbleting, Luptee lugana.

Girt, Khoob hoodara.

Girt line, *Gatlin*.

Glass (*hour*), G,huree kee sheeshee. *(spy)*, Doorbeen *or* doormeen, *(a night)*, Rat ka doormeen.

To flog or sweat the glass, Wuqt hoo,a nuheen, sheeshee p,hirana.

Googings, Sookan ka madu.

Goose neck, Nor *boom* ka *hook*. *Wings of a sail*. (*)

(*) I have not been so fortunate as to get a term for this, neither do I believe there exists one among the lascars; except it be, *bura pirmun uor trikut pirmun ka las k,hoola*.

Goring cloth, Tirsa, kulee.

Grape shot, *Gerub ch,haut.*

Grapling or grapnel, *Griblee, grafin.*

Gratings, P,halke kee jalee.

Graving, *Boordoo men* booch g,husna.

Grenado or hand grenades, Tonta *or tata*.

Gripes, *Lang* ka lubran.

Griping, *Baksee* aneko chahna, gos jane mangna.

Grog, *grag.*

Gromet, *Girmut.*

Grounding, Sook,he pur lugna.

Ground tackle, Nungur ka surunjan *or* surumjam (*properly* surunjam).

Guard boat, Chuokee ka muchwa. *Ship*, Chuokee wala juhaz.

Guess or guest rope, Pagur.

Gulf, Goob,h.

Gun, Top. *See Cannon, musket.* (*evening*), Rat kee top, at,h g,huree ka top. (*morning*), Fujur kee top, goriya por ka top, g,huriya por ka top.

Gun boat, *Gun bot*. *Carriage*, Top kee garee. *Powder*, Baroot, daroo. *Shot*, Gole ka tuppa. *Tackles*, Top ka luptee.

Gunnel (*of a boat*), Mez *or* Mench.

Gunner, *Guner.*

Gunners's mate, *Guner* ka *met.*

Gunnery, Goolumdaree (*which ought to be go*lundazee).

Gust, J,hupeta, d,hupa.

Guy, *G,hu,ee*. *For the boom*, *Boom g,hu,ee*. (*A rope extending from the main mast to fore mast*), Mat *g,hu,ee*.

To gybe, *Boom* ka serh p,hirana.

H.

To hail, Boongul se bat kurna.

Half pike, B,hala. *See Boarding pikes*.

Haliards, Hunja.(*)

Hammer, Martil,(**) murtil, hut,horee.

Hammock, Jolee, j,holee, j,hoolee.

Hand, Admee, khulasee. (*All hands*), Sub admee, sub khulasee. *Grenade*, Tota, tonta. *Lead*, Hat,h proom, ch,ho*t*a proom. *Over hand* (*quickly*), Lug girgir, hat,ho*n* hat,h, juldee. *Pump*, Ch,ho*t*a bumba, hat,h bumba. *Spike*, *Hanspeek*.

To hand the sail, Ser,h lupe*t*na, ser,h band,hna.

Handsomely, Aste aste (*properly*) ahiste ahiste.

To hang as a mast, Te*r*ha ho jana.

To hang on a rope, Hat,ho*n* hat,h hoodarna.

To go hank for hank, Dono burabur heriya marna uor burabur chulna.

Hanks, Suwa,ee ke ku*r*e, *huk*.

Harbour, Bundur, bin-

(*) Corrupted by Europeans to hanjes and anjes!
(**) *Port.* Martello.

dur, g,hat.

Harbour master, G,hat Cuptan.

Harpings, P,haltoo chuplan.

Harpoon, Ek dant wala kawur.

Harpooner, Soos mar, soos marne wala.

Hatch or hatch way, P,halka *or* falka. (*After hatch way*), Kilmee p,halka, kulmee falka. (*Fore hatch way*), Trikut p,halka. (*Main hatch way*,) Bura p,halka, bura falka.

Hatch bars, P,halke ke putte.

Hatches, P,halke ka kewar, falke ka duwazu.

Hatchet, Koowaree, kooralee.

To haul, Lugna, lagna, tanna. (*Sometimes* k,huench lena *is used*).

To haul the wind, Huwa kee turuf p,hir jana.

Hawse, Do nungur. (*Foul hawse*), Humar men bolta. *Bags*, Ank,h ka booch. *Holes*, Juhaz ka ank,h, (*properly* juhaz kee ank,h). *Pieces*.

Hawser, Ch,hota humar, *hansil*.

Heap (*ornamental figure*), Pootla, moorut. (*Of a ship*), Anee, unee, sir, mat,ha. (*Literally, the forehead*). (*Of a mast*), Kalsir, kalsur. *Fast*, Agil ka pagur. *Land*, Tek wala ponta. *Rope*, Mutwar ka (kee) alat. *Sails*,

Agil ka ser,h. *Sea*, Agil ka muoj. *Stick*, Lukree kee teemlee. *Wind*, Agil ka huwa.

By the head, Agil b,haree.

To have head way, Agil bur,hna.

Headmost ship, Agil juhaz.

Heart, Suwa,ee ka mutam.

To heave a head, Pagur band,hke age tanna.

To heave a stern, Pagur band,hke peech,he tanna.

To heave down, Juhaz ko wura kurna, *heel* kurna.

To heave the lead, Proom dalna. *See the phrase*, *Heave the lead.*

To heave round, Hubesna.

To heave short, Hubesna *peek.*

To heave in stays, Suwa,ee neeche tanna.

To heave taught, Hubesna *tat.*

To heave out, Saf kurna, k,hal dena.

To heave keel out, Put,han (eraf) dek,hne waste wura kurna.

Heaver, Neepur.

A heavy sea, Ak,hree durya, gurm durya.

Heel, Sookan kee d,har. (*Of a mast*), Poondul, foondul.

To heel, *Heel* kurna, kurwut ho-jana, numna.

Helm (*of a ship*), Sookkan. (*The word* putwal *or* putwar, *is used by the fresh water lascars about Chutganw*).

Helmsman, Sookkanee, (*whence perhaps the*

word a Seacunnie).

Hide (*for service*), Chumroo.

High and dry, Ek dum sook,he pur chur buet,ha.

High sea, Bura bura d,hem muoja, bure bure luhur. *Water*, B,hurpoor. *See Flood.* *Water mark*, B,hurpoor ka *marka*.

Hitch, *Heench*. (*Blackwall hitch*), Sunjal ketlee, wilatee ketlee, (*literally, the European hitch.*) *The term* hook heench *is used by the Bengal lascars*. (*Racking hitch*), Ketlee (*Rolling hitch*), Rook,ha punsee *heench*), *Timber hitch*), Chut put ka *heench*.

To hich, *Heench* marna.

Hoase or hose, Kebee.

Hoay, Ure.

To hoist, Hukarna. *

Hold, K,hun, k,hunr. (*After hold*), Kilmee p,halke ka k,hun, peech,hil ka k,hun. (*Fore hold*), Trikut p,halke ka k,hun. (*Main hold*), Bure p,halke ka k,hun. (*Grasp*), Pukur.

To rummage the hold, K,hun men d,hoodh,na.

To stow the hold, K,hun ka mal k,humal kurna.

To hold on, Hoodarna.

To hold the water, Las kurna.

Holders, K,hun wale.

(*) Pronounced often by European *ankarna*.

Holding water, Panee pukurna.

Holloa, B,hula b,hula, han hue.

To haul home, Chikar tanna. *The fore, main, mizen, and jib sheets*, Chikar lugna. *All other sheets*, Chikar champna.

To come home (as spoken of the anchor), Kusur kurna.

Home-bound ships, Upne moolk jane wale juhaz.

Hommoc, Tekra.

Hood, P,halkee kee petee. (*Of the galley chimney*), Chooldan ke nul ka d,hukna. (*Of a pump*). Boombe ka d,hukna. (*Navel hoods or whoods*), Ank,h kee girmut.

Hook, *Hook*, qoolab *is more used by the Arabs than by the Indians.* (*For fish*), Gul. (*Laying hook*, Churkhee ka *hook*.

To hook on, *Hook* lugana.

Horizon, Asman ka d,har.

Horse, Tunee, tunnee. (*Flemish*), P,haltoo tunee. (*For hoisting yards, &c.*, *Tapproos, tafruk.*

Hose, Kebee. *See hoase.*

Hounds, Danga.

Housed, Band,hela (top.)

Housing or house line, Mug jee ka len.

Hoy, *Bot*. (*Although this word is evidently a corruption of boat, it is never used, I believe, for such, but instead of it* muchwa.) *See Boat.*

To hug the land, Kinare ke chikar jana, kinare nuzdeek jana.

To hug the wind, Huwa ke moon*h* men jana.

Hulk (a), Ka,in. (*Sheer*) *Hel bot.*

Hull, Moon*d*a juhaz, loon*d*a juhaz, *down,* Khalee ser,h dol nuzur ate hue.' *To,* Nungurwaree be burabur nuzur ata hue.

To hull a ship, Boordoo men marna.

Hurricane, Charon turuf ka ek dum toofan.

Husband (ship's), Juhaz ka khawind.

I—J

In (furled), Band,hela.

Inch, Heench, * tussoo, booral.

Insurance, Beema, veema.

Iron work, Lohe ka kam. *Sick,* Lohe ka kam batil hoo,a, kut k,ha guya.

Island or isle, Tapoo, junjeera (*a corruption of* juzeera).

Jack, Jug. Block, Jug boolak. In the bread room, in country ships, the person who takes care of the provisions, etc. of the ship, is called kusub *or* kusuf, *a Jack of all trades.*

Jack in the box, Doom khulas ka nur.

To jam, Jam ana, *jam* hona *or* kurna.

Jears, Mat yaree.

(*) This word signifies also a hitch.

Jetty-head.

Jewel blocks, Dustoor hunja ke las kee kupoe.

Jib * *Jeeb* (*Flying*), *P,hulane jeeb.* (*Middle*), P,haltoo *jeeb,* *Boom,* *Jeeb boom.* *Flying,* *P,hulane jeeb* ka *boom.* *Sheet,* *Jeeb* damun.

Jibing, *See, to gybe.*

Jigger, Mat kee luptee.

Jigger (*fleet*), *Fleet* kee luptee. *Tackle,* Sat,hiya luptee.

Jolly boat, Jalee bot.

Journal, Juhaz ka roznamu.

Jumper, *J,hampur.* Sat,h *is used by the Bengal lascars.*

Junk, Joong.

Jury mast, P,haltoo *dol,* faltoo *dol.*

K.

To keckle, Humar ko p,hural kurna.

Kedge, Lot,haree nungur. *See Anchor.*

Keel, Put,han, erab, eraf. (*Even*), Seed,ha put,han, erab burabur. (*False*) P,haltoo put,han, *keelnee,* *sookan* *k,heela.*

Keelson, Undur ka put,han.

To keep away, Damun ruk,hna.

To keep land aboard, Kinare *suee* kurkur jana, kinare undeet,h hokur nuheen jana.

To keep off the shore or land, Kinare se bahur

* There is an other jib, the name of which at present I have forgot in English, which the lascars call *Shuetan jeeb,* the devil's jib.

ruk,hna.

To keep full, B,hurriya ruk,hna.

To keep the luff, Gos ruk,hna, gos jana.

Keeper (*boat keeper*) Muchwe ka p,huliya, ful wala, *used by the Bengal lascars.*

Kentledge, Lohe ka *ketlee* neerum (leelum) ke waste. (*limber kentledge of lead*) Seense (sheeshe) kee pat neerum ke waste.

Ketch, Der,h gosee.

Kevel, Mankree. *Heads*, Mankree.

Key (*quay*), Dunka, band,hela g,hat, puka g,hat.

Kink, G,huree.

Knee, Bank, kurwa, kurva, kafinna. (*Of the head*) *See Cut water. Knees* (*dagger*). (*Hanging*), Tenchin. (*Iron*). Lohe ka bank. (*lodging*). (*standard*). (*Transom*). *See Transom.*

Knight heads, Subdre kee moot.

Knittles, Netlee *or* netliyan.

To knock off, Kam ek dum ch,hor dena.

Knot, Giruh. (*Bow line*), Damunee *heench*. (*Double wall*), Doobral bosu giruh, (*single wall*), Sunjul bosu, chukree.

(*Over hand*), Suluk giruh.

(*Reef*), Seed,hee giruh.

(*Shroud*), Lubranee giruh.

(*Stopper*), Chukree giruh, bosu giruh.

Knot (*of the log line*), Tup ke *len* ke *marke* ka giruh.

L.

*To labour** (*as a ship*).

Ladder, Seer,hee. (*Stern*), Duboose kee seer,hee.

Laden, B,hurela, b,hur chooka.

Ladle, Gole nikalne ka chumuch. (*Paying*), Damun *d*alne ka chumuch.

Laid up (*for want of employment, etc.*) Tuwa,e pura. (*When from age, and unfit for further service*), Poorana *t*,heekra hoo,a.

Lake, J,heel.

Lake (*formed by art*), Tula,o, pok,hur.

Land, Kinaru, tur.

Land breeze, Turiya huwa, kinare ka huwa. *Fall*, Puela kinaru jo nuzur aya. *Lock*, Goob,h ke undur bundur.

To make the land, Kinare dek,hna.

Landsman, Kinare wala.

Langrel or langrage, Kirch ka gola.

Laniard, G,hora, g,hoorla.

Laniards of the stoppers, Bose ke s,ath. *See Stoppers.*

Lantern, Fanoos *or* p,hanoos.

Lap sided, *Boordoo* j,hookta.

Larboard, Dawa *boordoo*. *Tack*, Dawee manch.

* I have not been able to get a term which corresponds with the above word. *See, To pitch and roll.*

To sail large, Ch,hoot damun chulna, *or* ket pur moora ruk,hna, *or* lurga *boolin* ruk,hna.

Lascar, a, Khulasee, k,harwa, k,haroo,a.

Lascar's plate for eating off, T,halee, rikabee, rikebee. (*Of wood*), Tuporee. *If a large wooden plate containing food for at least 10 or 12 men*, k,hooncha, (*properly* k,hwoanchu).

Lashing, *Lasun*.

To lash, *Lasun* lena, *istop* band,hna.

Lastage, Neelum, neerum, *or* leelam.

Lateen sail, Kolee ser,h.

To launch, Juhaz *ootar*na.

To lay the land, Jank,ha jank,ha dek,hna.

To lay in off a yard arm, *Las* men se undur ana.

To lay out on a yard arm, *Las* men bahur jana.

Lead, Proom. (*Deep sea*), Bura proom.

To heave the lead, Proom *d*alna.

Leading wind, Danw kee huwa.

Leadsman, Proom *d*alne wala.

League, Der,h kos.*

Leak, Soolak, ch,hed.

To leak, Choona.

To spring a leak, Gamut hona *or boomba* hona.

Leakage, Choo,ak.

Leaky, Buhoot gamtee.

* *Der,h* signifies one and half; and one *kos* is two miles.

To leave off, Ch,hor jana, ch,hor dena.

Ledge Khurabu, chur, chura.

Ledges, Perche, kata baree.

Lee, B,hare, huwa ke neeche.

Lee boards, P,haltoo sookan. *Lurch*, B,hare j,hook. *Side*, B,haree turuf, b,hare boordoo. *Shore*, B,hare men kinaru. *Tide*, B,hare duriya ka tan. *Way*, B,hare pura.

To make lee way, B,hare purna, b,hare jana.

Under the lee, Asre men.

Leeches, Het,hee. heent,hee.

Leech lines, Seeseedor, seezador. *(Harbour)*, Gave ka seeseedor.

Rope, Bar kee het,hee kee alad.

To lengthen, Lumba kurna.

To let in, Sand,hna, jor lugana.

To let out a reef, *Reef* ch,hor dena.

To leward, B,haree turuf.

Leward ship, B,hare chulne wala juhaz.

To lie along or over, Wura ho ruhna, kurwut ko ruhna.

To lie to, Ara parna, k,hob,hurna.

To lie well up, Khoob gos chulna.

Lifts, Mutela, mantela, munteela, muntel. *(Topping)*, *See Topping.*

Light (a candle), Buttee. *(In weight,)* Hulka.

To light (to help), Mud-ud dena.

Lighter (at Bombay), Puruo, horee. (*At Calcutta*), Bhur, *suloop*. (*At China*), Ch,hab. (*At Madras*), Chiling. (*Covered or close*), Ola, putiya, tootuk wula horee. (*Ballast lighter*), Neerum ka b,hur.

Light house, Kundeeliya,* butteekamoonaru.

Lights (floating), Khurabu kee buttee.

Limber boards, Put,har ka tagur. *Hole*, Sungra, (*plural*) sungre. Bank boornal *is used by the Bengal lascars.* *Kentledge, See Kentledge.*

Line, Paj, kutar (*properly* qutar).

Line, concluding line, Beech ka ch,hera, beech ka ch,hura. (*Deep sea*), Bura proom ka *len*. (*Fishing*), Much,hee ka *dor*, gul kee *doree*. (*Hand*), Hat,h proom ka *len*. (*Hauling*), *Gatleen* kee alat. (*Life*), Chal kee alat. (*Mar line*), Do panee russee, do panee alad. (*Navel*), Sar ke *istap*, sar kee jolee. (*Spilling*), Surera. surela.

List, Numun, j,hooka,o.

To load (a gun), Top b,hurna. (*A ship*), juhaz b,hurna.

Loading of a ship,

* From *qundeel*, a candle, lantern, &c.

Boj,hu,ee.

Log, Tup.

Log-board, Tup kee tukhtee. *Book*, Tup-namu. *Line*, Tup ka *len*.

Log-reel, Tup kee churkhee.

Loggerhead, *Tar* (damur) gurum kurne ka gola.

Long boat, *See Boat*.

Long hawse, Samur.

Loom of an oar, *See Oar*.

To loose, Ch,hor dena.

To loose a rope, Alat ch,hor dena. alat k,hol dena.

Lost, Mara guya, *doob* guya, buet,h guya, gharut hoo,a, sulamut hoo,a. (**)

To be lost, Mara jana.

Low water, Ka,im (*properly* qa,im) panee. (*If in a river*), Sar b,hat,ha. *See Tide*.

To lower, Uriya kurna.

Lower trussel-trees, Koorsee.

Lubber, Dandee, koolee, motiya.

Lubber's hole. Panjre ka gala.

Luff tackle, Kuturnal.

To luff, Gos jana, gos ana.

Lugger.

Lug sail, Do gosee ser,h, punk,hee ser,h.

Lug sail boat, Punk,hee ser,h wala muchwa.

Lumpers, B,hutte wale.

Lurch, *See Lee lurch*.

Lying to, K,hob,hurta.

** It is singular, that the literal meaning of this term is *saved*, and in which sense it may also be taken.

To lie to, K,hob,hurna,* *baksee* k,hura ruhna. (*To wait for*), Rah dek,hna.

M.

Magazine, B,haroot khanu.

Magnet, Chumuk put,-hur, jeeta loha, (*literally, living iron*). *See Compass.*

Main, Bura. *Brace*, Bura *buras*. *Tackle*, Bura mat yaree.

To make, Bunana, kurna. *See Sail.*

To make a good board, Uch,ha manch jana, uch,ha gos jana.

To make the land, Kinaru dek,hna.

To make sail, Ser,h kurna. (**)

To make stern way, Peech,he purna, peech,he hutna.

To make water, Gamut kurna, gamut hona, panee lena, panee kurna.

Mallet, Mogree, mongree. (*Calking*), Kulpat kee mogree. (*Serving*), Fral (frar) kee mogree.

Man rope, *Boordoo* ka ch,hora.

To man, Tueyar ruhna, tueyar ruk,hna, hat,h men ruk,hna.

* *K,hob,hurna* appears to be the proper word as used by the lascars of Bombay, Surat, and *G,hog,ha*, *&c.* although, perhaps, not understood by the lascars of Bengal, who, however, have adopted most of the terms used by the former, and are (by every thing that I can learn) far inferior sailors.

** The idiom of the two languages perfectly agrees in this term.

To man a prize, Pukurela juhaz men admee ruk,hna.

To man ship, *Hoorra* (*or* sulamee) dene ko khulasee tueyar ruk,hna, sulamee dene ko pirmum ke oopur jana, sulamee dene ko lubran pur jana.

Manger board, Ank,h ka tukhtu.

Manifest, Mal ka hisabnamu.

Marine board, Juhaz ke *kuonsul*.

Mariner, Durya wutee, durya wurdee.

Marines, Juhaz ke sipahee (*literally*, *ship soldiers*).

Maritime, Durya,ee.

Marline, *See Line*.

Marling, Kawuree.

Spike, Pasador. (*)

To marry two ropes, Pulas kurna. *See to splice*.

Martingale, Mutun g,hu,ee, mutun ga,ee. *Perhaps corruptions of the English word*.

Mast, Dol (**) (*Lambs-*

---

* In Portuguese the word *passador* signifies a bolt, also a maring pike.

** Permit me in this place to inform the reader, that by prefixing the words *trikut*, pronounced also *trikut* fore, *bura* main, and *kilmee* or *kulmee* mizen, any phrase required may be formed, as *trikut gavee dol* the fore top mast; *burasubur* the main top gallant sail, and *kilmee tubur* the mizen royal. Let it be also observed, that lascars, in speaking of the different sails, seldom add the words *ser,h* or *sur*, signifying sail, except to the main-sail, which is called *bura ser,h*; therefore the main top sail is called *bura gavee*, instead of *bura gavee ser,h*.

men use the word mustool.)

Mast (fore), Tirkut dol, trikut dol. *(Jury)*, *See Jury.* *(Made)*, Chupul wala dol, sande wala dol. chapus wala dol. *(Main)*, Bura dol. *(Mizen)*, Kilmee dol, kulmee dol. *(Rough)*, Sonta *or* sota dol bunane la,iq, *literally, a spar fit for making a mast)*. *(Top)*, Gavee dol. *(Top gallant)*, Subur dol, subur koondu. *(Top gallant royal)*, Tubur dol, tubur koondu.

To mast a ship, Dol lena, dol k,hura kurna.

Master of a ship, *See Captain.*

Master attendant, G,hat *Kuptan.*

Mat, Godree.

Match, Jamgrec, jamgee, jamkee.

Mate (of a ship), Malum, *a corruption of the Arabic word*, moo,ullim *an instructor, pilot, etc.* *(An assistant)*, *Met.*

Maul (top), *Tup mal.*

Mess (of the lascars), Vecsiya, beesiya.

Mess mate, Weesc wala, beesiya.

Messenger, *Masindur.*

Mid channel, K,haree ke beech, becch d,har, munj d,har. *Ship*, Beech men. *Ship beam*, Beech ka *beem*, beech ka baree. *Ship frame*, Beech ka *furma.*

Midshipmen, *Beechmen, meechilmen.*

Mid ships, Juhaz ka

beech.

Mizen, Kilmee *or* kulmee. *Mast*, Kulmee dol. *See Mast.*

Vangs, Turnal.

Moon, Chand. Qumur *is used by the Arabs.*

Moon raker, Lubur.

To moor, Char pugree kurna, char pukuree kurna. *A cable each way*, Do nungree kurna, do lungree kurna. *Head and stern*, Agil peechˌhil ka do nungree kurna. *With a spring upon the cable*, Duboose ka pagur ara parna.

Moorings, Boye.

Mortar, Huwaˌe, ookˌhlee, kotˌhee top.

Mortice (a), Kˌhabul.

Mould, Map.

Mounted (as a gun), Garee pur churela.

To mount, Churana, churˌhana.

Mouse, Hunrum *mooch*, suwaˌee ka unarus, suwaˌee ka unnus. (*)

To mouse a hook, Hook ko galbund bandˌhna.

To muffle the oars, Huleese ko firal lugana.

Musket, Bundook (*properly* bundooq).

Muster Gintee, haziree, hajiree.

To muster, Haziree lena, gintee lena.

Mutineer, Dunguˌee, fusadee, mootfurnee (*a corruption of* mootuffunee).

Mutiny, Dunga, fusad.

To mutiny, Dunga kurna, fusad kurna.

* Literally, the pine-apple of the stay; *unnus* is a corruption of *ununnas*, a pine-apple.

N.

Nader, Putal.

Naval, Juhazee, durya wutee, durya wurdee.

Navel whoods, *See Hoods*. *Line*, *See Line*.

Navigation, Juhazee ilm, juhazee hikmut.

Navigator, Juhaz chulane wala, durya ka hisab ruk,hne wala, malum. *See Pilot*, *Mate*.

Navy (*fleet*), Juhazon kee fuoj, kapla, kafila. (*)

Nautical, Juhazee.

Neap tides, B,hang ka juwar, mur kutal, murukutal.

Neaped, Sook,he men luga.

Needle, *See Compass*. (*Bolt rope*), Het,hee seene ka soo,a, neengur kurne ka soo,a.

Needles (*sail*), Ser,h seene ka soo,a.

Netting, Jalee. *See Boarding*. (*Over head*), Ch,hutree kee jalee.

Nettles, *See Knittles*.

Night, Rat. *Night and day*), Rat-din.

To nip, *Neep* lena.

Nippers, *Neepur*. (*Selvage*), *Sewajee* ka *neepur*.

Nipper men, *Neepur* band,hne wale.

No man's land, *Habeet* ka gala.

Norman, Duor ka moot.

North, Oottur, ga,ee, shimal. *This last word is used by the*

* From *qafilu*, a body of travellers, a caravan, &c.

Arabs. East, Eesan kona, nishan kona, ga,ee mutulue ukurub. *West*, Agnee kona, b,hundar, kibku,e jimna ukubub. *See West.*

Northward, Oottur turuf, ga,ee turuf.

North wind, Oottura huwa, ga,ee ba,o.

Nuts of an anchor, *See Anchor.*

O.

Oakum, Istoob, istup. (*) *White*, Sufed istoob.

Oar, Hulesa, dand. *The blade*, P,hun, putta. *The hand*, Moot,h. *The loom, Dandee.*

Oars, double banked, *See Banks.*

To hoat the oars, Helan kurna.

To ship the oars, Hulesa *d*alna.

Observation.

Off, near, Nuzdeek.

Off and on, Ata jata.

Officer, of a ship, Malum. *See Mate. Of the watch*, Por ka malum.

Offing, Bahur, *often called* bar *by the lascars.*

Open, as harbour, K,hoolasa, (bundur.)

Opening, Gala.

Order, Hookm, mudar. *This last word properly signifies a task, charge.*

Order of sailing, Juhaz chulane ka hookm.

Ordinary seamen, Ad,ha khulasee. (**) *Ships*

* *Port.* Estopa.— ** Literally, a half seaman.

in, Tuwu,ee pura juhaz, tuwu,ee ruha juhaz.

Orlop, Humat ka bich,hana.

Over board, Durya men gira. *Cast*, Budlee churela. *Masted*, Dol buhoot b,haree.

To over haul, Milana, saf kurna. *To examine*, Tulash kurna.

To over haul, to search among the lascars' chests for any thing stolen, J,hara lena.

To over set, Oond,ha kur dena.

Out fit, Khurch, khurj.

Out rigger, a small boom, Panjre kee dewee.

Out of sight, Undeet,h.

To out sail, Surus chulna, ziyadu chulna.

To be out of trim, Soost hona. (*) *Literally, to be lazy or slow.*

Owner, Juhaz ka d,hunee, juhaz ka malik.

P.

Packet, *Paket*, qasid ka juhaz.

Paddle, Hat,h hulesa, chumchu, pungue, buet,ha, *used by the natives of Bengal, it is derived from* buet'h-na, *to sit down.*

Painter, a rope, Muchwe ka pagur. *Shank painter*, *See*, *Shank*.

Palm, Ser,h seene kee hut,heree.

Panch, Bura godree, p,hool ka godree.

Parbuckle, J,hoolee.

* The lascars seem to be at a loss for a term.

Parceling, Pasleen.

Parceling a seam, Wadre ko *pasleen* lugana.

Parrel, Luddoo wala sar.*

Parrel rope, Do ank'h ka sar.

Parrel with ribs, etc., Luddoo wala mankree uor sar, luddoo wala bustar. *Truss parrel,* Yaree ka sar.

Parsling, See Parceling.

To part (as a ship). Humar tor kur jana, kumar *toot* jana.

Partners, Chupul p,han*t*a, ch,hed, chapus.

Pass or passport, Ruwanu, purwanu.

To pass along, Ek doosre ko dena, hat,h lena, hat,h se hat,h dena. (*To take a turn of a rope),* Bolta lena, bolta hoodarna.

Passage, Mat,ha. *See Voyage.*

Passage boat. Turee par hone ka muchwa.

Passaree, Mooree ka sat.

Passenger, Ootaroo, *pasender.*

Paunch, P,hool ka godree. *See Panch.*

Pawl, Pal.

Pawl bits, Pal panw, *pal* k,hooree.

To pay (daub), Rung lugana.

To pay a mast or yard, Juhaz ke dol me*n* churbee lugana.

To pay away or out,

* *Luddoo* means a truck

Tirkana.

To pay a seam, Istoob kurna. *See Oakum.*

To pay off, Damum jana.

To pay off (discharge), Tulub dekur wida kurna, juwab dena.

Peak, Koona, *peek*.

Peak haliards, Bat ka hunja, *peek* hunja.

Pendant (flag), Ma,ee. (*Broad pendant*), Kutwel, purera, fureta. *(rudder pendant)*, Sookan ka mat. (*a short piece of rope*), Mat, mad.

Pier, Dunka, pukka g,hat, pench ka g,hat.

Pig of ballast (iron), Ketlee. (*Lead*), Pat.

Pike, Burch,hee, b,hala.

Pilot, Urkatee.*

Pilot (at Surat), Doongvee. (*among the Arabs*), Rooban.

Pin of a block, Kupee kee chabee.

Pins (belaying), Tol, toolit.

Pinnace, *P,hineez*.

Pintles, Nur.**

Pirate (ship), Chanchiya juhaz, *this term is used by the Bombay lascars*, dukuet ka juhaz, chor ka juhaz, kund,haree juhaz.

Piracy, Dukuetee, choree.

Piss dale, Peshab ka boornal, peshab ka

* It is supposed they got this name from the only Pilots formerly in this part of the world, being in the service of the Nuwwab of Urkat *(Arcot)*.

** Literally, the male.

purnal.

Pitch, Dàmur, *peech,h*.

To pitch (*as a ship*), Mat,ha marna.

To pitch the seams, Damur lugana.

Pistol, Tubunchu, *pistuol*.

Plane (*an instrument*), Ronda, runda.

Plank, Tukhtu, patiyoon.*

To plank, Tukhtu lugana.

To plait, Seekee bunana, goont,hna.

Plat (*for serring cables*), Tannasa, tanoosa. *Perhaps from the Portuguese*, trancas.

Platform, Purancha.**

Plate, Lohe ka putta. (*Back stay*), Pet furodee ka putta. (*futtock or foot hook*), Putuk lubran ka *hook*.

Pleasure boat, Suwaree ka muchwa.

Plug, Sho,era, cho,era dutta, mekh, booch, *kak* (*from cork*) pina.

To plug up a shot hole, Booch marna, dutta marna, sho,eramarna.

Plugs (*hawse*), Ank,h booch.

Plunder, Loo*t*.

To plunder, Loo*t*-a-loo*t* kurna, loo*t* lena.

To be plundered, Loo*t*a jana, Loo*t*a ho-jana.

To ply, Ba,o kee turuf qusd kurkur jana.

Point, Tek, ponta. (*Head land*), Ponta. (***) *Blank*, Seed,ha.

* *Patiyoon*, is much used by the lascars from *G'hog'ha*.

** In Portuguese *prancha* means a plank, stage, float, etc.

*** In Portuguese *ponta* signifies a point or headland.

To point, Ga,e doom kurna, *or* pota *pooten* kurna. (*A gun*), Moojra lena, moojra ruk,hna, sad,hna.

To point (*a sail*), *Reef* ka seekee b,hurna.

Points, Seekee.

Pole axe, Kooharee, tubur.

Pole mast, Sub ser,h band,hela.

Poles (*under bare*), *Ringeen* pur. (**)

Poop, Ch,hutree.

To poop, Duboose tor dalna.

To be pooped, Duboosu *toot* jana.

Pooping sea, a, Dubose torne ka muoja.

Port, Bindur, bundur.

Bars, Baree kee lukree.

Portlid, Baree ka durwazu.

Port ropes, Baree ka ch,hena.

Port tackles, Baree kee luptee.

Ports, K,hirkee, baree, (*Middle deck*), Beech ke tootuk kee k,hirkee. (*Lower deck*), Neeche ke tootuk kee k,hirkee.

Press of sail, Tesum t,hes hukarela, mate mat hukarela.

Press'd man, Begaree pukurela, d,hunnee ka khulasee, d,hurnee ka khulasee.

Press gang, D,hurnee

** The lascars, instead of saying that the ship is sailing under bare poles, say that the ship is sailing by means of the rigging, (or the force the winds has upōn the rigging); therefore, they do not say, *juhaz nunge dol pur chulta hue,* but *juhaz ringeen pur chulta hue.*

kee tolee.

Preventer, P,haltoo, faltoo. *See Spare. Brace*, P,haltoo *bras. Shrouds*, P,haltoo lubran. *Stay*, P,haltoo suwa,ee. *Back stay*, Faltoo furodee.

Prick, *Rol*, pilindu. *Of tobacco*, *Tumbakoo* kee buttee.

Priming, Runjuk, kan.

Priming wire or iron, Seekh, soo,a.

Privateer, Chor ka juhaz, Chunchiya ka gulwut, *a name given to a pirate.*

Prize, Quedee juhaz, pukurela juhaz.

To prize, *raise*, Veendee kurna, beendee kurna, champnee kurna.

Prize money, Inam ka puesa, k,hant puesa, *or* jeetela puesa.

Promontory, Ponta, tek, unee.

Protest, Mal ke nooqsan kee chittee.

Pudding for a boat, *Hans*, muchwe ka hans, dufra, hanslee.

Pulley, *a*, Gireree, girelee, goorgoora. *This last word is used by the Bengal lascars.*

To pull, Lugna, lagna, tanna, k,huenchna.

Pump, Bumba.*

To pump, Bumba champna.

Pump bolt, Bumbe ka techin. *Box*, Bumbe kee palee. *Brake*, Bumbe ka lat,h. *Dales*, Bumbe ka nul.

* *Port.* Bomba.

Gear, Bumbe ke surunjam. *Hood*, Bumbe ka d,hukna. *Hook*, Bumbe ka *hook*. *Hose*, Bumbe kee kebee. *Leather*, Bumbe ka chumra. *Sounding rod*, Bumbe ka seekh. *Spear*, Bumbe ka lumba jooj. *Tacks*, Bumbe ka preg.*

Punt, Doonga, t,hapura, deengee.

Purchase, *price*, Khureed, dam, mol. *Power*, Kul, hikmut.

To purchase, Mol lena, khureed kurna.

Purser, Juhaz ka kiranee, P*usur*. *Purser's steward*, P*usur* ka met, *Istoor*.

Q.

Quadrant, Kuman.

Quarantine, Kinare ane ka ut,hka,o.

Quarter, Chutree ka boordoo. *On the*, Chutree ke burabur boordoo men. *Bill*, Haziree ka kaghuz, upnee juguh juguh ka kaghuz. *Cloths*, Boordoo ka purdu. *Deck*, *See Deck*. *Gallery*, Set khanu, qundeel. *Master*, *Kot mastur*. *Netting*, *See Netting*. *Quarter!* Khooda ke waste moo,af kur! *Rails*, Boordoo ka *rel*. *Tackle*, Bura lasyaree.

To ask for quarter, Punah mangna, moo,af mangna.

Quartering wind, Kilmee (mez) mej bura-

* *Port.* Prego.

bur huwa.

Quarters, Upnee upnee juguh juguh.*

Quarters of the yards, Las.

Quay, *See Key.*

Quick sand, Chor baloo, duldul zumeen, lub lubee zumeen.

Quick work, Dubela, buet,hela.

Quoin, Mojura patlee.

Quoins, Kooniyan.

R.

Rabbit, K,hampnee.

Race, Panee ka tan.

Rack, Alat b,hurne kee patlee.

To rack, a tackle, Yaree *neep* lena.

Raft, Purancha, trapa. *Port*, Lukree lene kee k,hirkee, tukhtu lene ka baree.

Rag bolt, Katela kubeelu, katela kuveela.

Rails, *Rel*, percha.**

To raise, lift, Oot,hana, utrung kurna.

Rake, Duboose ka merab. *Of a mast, if towards the side*, Numun. *If fore or aft*, J,hamp.

To rake, as a mast, J,hoomna, j,hookna.

To rake, Duboose men jake k,hure gola marna, agul men jake k,hure gola marna.

Rammer or ramrod, of a musket, Guz. *Of a cannon*, Soomba, ch,humba.

Random shot, Be-muzoora gola, ooran gola.

Range, of shot, Gole ka

* Respective stations.— ** *Port.* Perchas, the rails of the head.

tuppa, gole ka pulla. *Of cable*, *Reench*.

To range, Kinaru b,heerkur ek suman chulana.

Rate.*

Ratlings, Iskat.**

To rattle down shrouds, Lubran men iskat band,hna, lubran ka iskat band,hna.

Reach, Bank.

Rear, *of a fleet*, *&c.*, Peech,hil wala juhaz.

Reckoning, *dead*, *See Dead*.

Reef, *of a sail*, *Reef*. *Of rock*, Danda, khurabu. *Band*, *Reef* kee putee. *Line*, *** Surera. *Tackle*, *Reef tanklee*, *reef teklee*.

To reef, *Reef* band,hna. *Cloose reefed*, Sub *reef* bandela, sub *reef* band,ha hoo,a.

Reel, Churkhee. *Deep sea*, Bura proom kee churkhee. *Log*, Tup kee churkhee. *Twine*, Sootlee bunane kee churkhee.

To refit, Muramut kurna, *properly* murummut kurna, sand,hna.

Reigning winds, Dustoor moowafiq huwa.

Relieving tackles, *for the tiller*, Sookan kee luptee.

To render, Saf hona, saf kurna.

Rendezvous, Juhaz moolaqat kee juguh.

* The lascars have no word corresponding with *rate*, at least I have not been so fortunate as to meet with it.

** *Port*. Escada, a ladder, also the ratlings of a ship.

*** I believe this small rope is not much used now-a-days.

Repair, Murummut.

To repair, Murummut kurna, sand,hna.

To repeat signals, Buota dek,hkur doosre ko dek,hana.

Repeating ship, Hookm puhoonchane wala juhaz.

Reprisal, to make, Pukurele ko pukurna.

To retreat, Peech,he hutna.

Ribbands, Sinta, sit.

Ribband, floor, Perche ka sit, perche ka sinta. *Breadth*, Kumurbund.

Ribs, of a ship, Juhaz ke are. *Of a parrel*, Sar kee mankree.

To ride, at anchor, Nungur pur hona, nungur baree men hona.

To ride, athwart, Huwa panee ke beech men nungur ware men ara hona. *Head to wind*, Huwa pur k,hura ruhna, huwa ke sam,hne sir ruk,hna. *Out a gale*, Toofan men hoodara ruhna. *Easy*, Aram se ruhna. *Hard*, Dook,h men ruhna.

A head rope of a sail, Luffa kurna.

Riders, Kes ka bank, koorma ka bank.

Ridge, of rocks, Chora put,hur, chora khurabu, chora junjeera. *See Reef.*

To rig, Ringeen tueyar kurna, map moowafiq bunana.

To rig in a boom, Boom undur tan lena.

To rig out a boom, Boom bar (*or* bahur)

hodee kurna.

Riggers, Ringeen kurne wale.

Rigging, Ringeen. Lower, Neeche ka *ringeen. Running,* Chaloo *ringeen,* chaloo alat. *Standing,* Jat,hoo *ringeen. Top mast,* Gavee *ringeen. Top gallant,* Subur *ringeen.*

Rigging loft, Bunsar, bunksal.

To right, as a ship, Seed,ha hona.

To right the helm, Sookan beech men ruk,hna, sookan seed,ha ruk,hna.

Rim or brim, Panjre ka d,har.

Ring bolt, Kura. *Ropes,* Tootuk ke kure ka bosu. *Tail, Drawul* dustoor. *Tail boom, Drawul* dustoor ka *boom.*

Ripling, Googanee, k,hulmulee.

Rising line.

Road or roadstead, Nungur waree, lungur baree.

Road, a good, Uch,ha bara.

Road, an open, K,hoola bara.

Roader or roadster, Nungur waree ka juhaz.

Robans or rope bands, Mutàr kee seekee.

Rocket, Huwa,ee.

Rock, a half tide, Ad,he b,hate ka put,hur.

Rocky, Put,hur kee juguh.

To roll, Ara lot marna.

Roller, Gureree roda.

Rollers, Rol, gurelee.

Rolling, Ara lot. *Hitch,*

Rol keench. Tackle, Rol tanklee.

Room, Juguh. *Bread,* Rotee khanu. *Cook, See Galley. Gun, See Gun. Sail,* Ser,h khanu, sur khanu. *Spirit,* Shurab khanu. *Store, Istor* khanu.

Rope bands, See Robands.

Rope house, Alat khanu.

Ropes, Alat. *Cable laid,* Koordumee alat. *Hawser laid,* Teen pan kee alat, teen pam kee alat.

Rope yarn, Roopiyan.

Rover. Chor juhaz.

Rough tree, Ungur,ha lukree, akha lukree.

Round house, Duboosa. *See Gallery.*

Rounding, Alat ka fural, *See Service.*

To round, Wutna, butna.

To round in, Hat,h b,hurna.

Round turn, Bolta. *Of the cables,* Humar ka poora bolta.

To rouse, the cable, Humar zor se lugna.

To row, Hulesa tanna.

Row lock, Tol ka gala.

Rowers, Hulese wala.

Row ports, Hulese kee k,hirkee, hulese kee baree.

Royal, Tubur. *See Mast, Yard, etc.*

Rudder, Sookan. *Chocks of,* Sookan ka chupula, sookan ka p,hanta. *Pendants,* Sookan ka mat.

Run, Juhaz ka peet,h ka moor,h, kilin.

Run, the distance sailed, Jam, duor. *Agree-*

ment, Iqrar, b,hund,-hun.

To run down a coast, Kinaru b,hirkur jana, g,huskur jana.

To run down a vessel, Chur,h buet,hna.

To run out the guns, Top ko bahur hodee kurna.

To run out a warp, Lumba pagur band,hna.

To let run a rope, Alat ek dum ch,hor dena.

Run-man, a, B,hagora. b,hagela.

Rung heads.

Runner, Mat wala yaree.

Running fight, B,hagtee lura,ee, b,hugelee lura,ee.

Running rigging, *See Rigging.*

Running part of a tackle, Yaree ka chaloo hat,h.

S.

Saddle, Tukiyu (*a prop, support, etc.*) *Of the bow sprit*), *Jeeb boom* ka tukiyu.

To sag to leeward, B,hare purna.

Sail, Ser,h, ser,h sur. *Loft*, Ser,h khanu, sur khanu. *Maker*, Ser,h seene wale ka sildar, ser,h seene wale ka sirdar, *silmagoor* ka misturee.

To set sail, Ser,h kurna.

To loose sail, Ser,h k,holna.

To make sail, Ser,h kurna.

To shorten sail, Ser,h k,hootana.

To strike sail, Ser,h uriya kurna.

To sail large, Lurga *boolin* ruk,hna. (*See To go free.*)

Sailer (a heavy), Unchaloo juhaz, uchaloo juhaz, kum chaloo juhaz. *(A prime)*, Bura chaloo juhaz.

Sailing (order of) Chulne ka dustoor.

Sailor, Khulasee, k,harwa,* duryawurdee. *(if an European)*, Gora khulasee. *(fresh water)*, Meet,ha panee ka khulasee, *dandee*. *(Used as terms of reproach)*.

Salute (from a ship or fort), Sulamee.

Sampane, Sampun, sumpan.

Samson post, Seer,hee ka *tenchun*.

Sand (island of), Baloo chur.

Saucer of the capstern, Duor ka t,halee.

To scale (cannon), (Top) ch,heekana, *(this term is only used by the lascars about Kutch and that part of India;)* top b,huk oorana *is used by the Bengalee lascars.*

Scant, Gosatee.

Scantling, Gol men.

To scarf, Sand,ha marna.

Scarfing, Sand,ha.

Schooner, Gosee wala juhaz, *Iskoonur*.

Scoop, Chumuch *(literally, a spoon)*, doonga.

Score (of a block, etc.), Wat.

Scraper, *Iskurap*.

Screen, Purdu.

To scrub the hammocks,

* *K,harwa* is much used by the lascars from Surat (Soorut), G,hog,ha, Sind, and Kutch.

J,holee g,husna, j,holee g,hus dena.

Scud, Budlee ka ch,hank, budlee kee nekree.

To scud, Toofan ke sat,h chulna.

Sculker, a, Gala k,hane wale,* uskutee.

Scull, Holee ka hulesa, ch,ho*t*a hulesa.

To scull, Holee marna.

Sculler, Holee marne wala.

Scuppers, Boornal. *Hoase*, Boornal kee kebee. *Nails*, Bura sir wala prek.* *Plugs*, Boornal ke d,hukne.

Scuttle, Ch,ho*t*a k,hirkee.

To scuttle (*a ship*), Juhaz ko gobree nikal kur *doo*ba dena.

Scuttle butt or cask, Chak wala peep.**

Sea, Durya, buhr. *The last word is used by the Arab sailors.* (*A long*), Lumba muoja. (*A short*), Toonka muoja, ch,ho*t*a muoja, g,huno muoja.

Sea boat, Toofan ke huk me*n* uch,ha juhaz. *Breeze*, Bar ka huwa. *Coast*, Durya ka kinaru. *Man* (*a sailor*), Khulasee, *called by Europeans* classee! *Legs*, Durya ka chal, durya kee chal. *Man or seafaring man*, Durya wutee, durya wurdee. *Mark*, Panee ka nisanee, panee ka *marka*.

Sea port, K,haree vina

* This appears to me fully to express the English term.
** *Port.* Prego.— *** *Port.* Pipas.

bindur, bin k,haree ka bundur. *Room,* Buhoot juhaz chulne ka muedan, durya ka bura muedan.
Weed, Durya ka kuchura, jurus, jur, put,hur ka j,har.

Seams, Kulasee, tukhte ka kustoora, tukhte ka d,har.

Seam (of canvas), Seewun, sila,ee.

Seine, Much,hee pukurne ka jal.

Seizing, Musalee.

To seize, Musalee band,hna.

Selvagee, Sevajee, selwajee.

Sending.

Sennit, Sinneet.

To serve, P,hural dena.

Service, P,hurar, p,hural, fular.

Serving mallet, Fural kee moogree.

To set (go, etc.), Jana.

To set sail, Ser,h kurna.

To set up, K,hurana, *tat* kurna.

To settle (lower), Uriya kurna. (*To sink as the deck, etc.,*) Buet,h jana. (*To ease off),* Tirkana.

Sextant, Kuman.

Shackles, Beree ka kura.

Shakes, Turuk, turuq, cheer, duru.

Shallop, Do dolee muchwa.

Shank, See Anchor.

Shank painter, Zunjeer wala bosu.

To shape a course, Munsoobe moowafiq juhaz chulana.

Sharp (to brace up), *Buras* chikar lugna.

Sheathing, P,hural.

Sheave, Roda.*

Sheave hole, Wat.

Sheepshank, Furodee kee ketlee.

Sheer, Panee d,hol.

To sheer, Boordoo b'heer kur chulana.

To sheer up a long side, Boordoo se boordoo burabur chulana.

To sheer off, Door b,hagna.

To break sheer.

Sheer hulk, Dol nikalne ka juhaz.

Sheering, Ar gos uwaree.

Sheers or shears, Kuturee.**

Sheet, Damun, daman, duman.

Sheet anchor, See Anchor.

To sheet home, Damun chikar champna.

Shell, Pocha gola, p,honka gola. (*Of a block*), Kupee ka gol, kupee gol.

Shelves, Danda, kada.

To shift, Budulna.

To shift a tackle, Yaree band,h ch,hor mil kurna. *See, To fleet.*

To shift the helm, Sookan ka bukra p,hirana.

To shift the messenger, Masindur p,hirana.

Shifted, Ek turuf p,hir guya.

Ship, Juhaz, wan,***

* In Portuguese the sheave of a block is called *Roda.*

** It is singular that *kuturee* in Hindoostanee is also the word for scissars.

*** Is often used by the lascars from Surat, G,hog,ha, Sind, Kutch, etc. but I am informed that the word is seldom if ever made use of by the Bengalees.

wahun.* (*Country, of India*), *Kutree* juhaz, moolkee juhaz, desee juhaz, moosulmanee juhaz. (*Cut down*), Tootuk ka*t*ela juhaz. (*Hospital*), *Ispeetal* ka juhaz. (*Merchant*), Suodaguree juhaz. (*Prison*), *Jel* khane ka juhaz, quedee ruk,hne ka juhaz.

Ship (receiving), D,hurum ka juhaz. (*Raised upon*), Tootuk bur,huela juhaz, *too*tuk undarela juhaz. (*Troop*), Fuoj lejane ka juhaz. *See Transport.*

Ship's company, Lushkur ka jut,ha, lushkur ka tolee lushkur ka mundulee, lushkur ka gol.

Ship master, *See Captain.*

To ship, Juhaz pur chur,hana. (*To fix*), Undur lugana, undur *d*alna.

To ship a sea, Muoj k,hana.

Shipping, Juhaz ka b,har, juhaz ka quafila, juhaz ka buhr.

Ship shape, Khulasee kee turuh.

To be shipwrecked, Pu*t*kun k,hana.

Shipwright, Juhaz ka mistree.

To shiver, Bujna, lup,hna, lufa marna.**

Shivering, Bujta, lup,hta.

Shoal, Baloo chura.

* In *Sunskrit*, Vahunu.
** The two last words perhaps come from the word *luff*.

Shoar, Gudum, gudam, k,humba.

Shoe of the anchor, Lungur ka * jootee, nungur kee jootee.

To shoe an anchor, Nungur ke dant ke neeche tukhtu ruk,hna.

To shoot a head, Agoo bur,hna, age bur,hna.

Shore, Kinaru, dara. *A bold,* Kinare chikar jane *d*ur nuhee*n*.

To shorten sail, Ser,h k,hootana.

Shot, Gola, golee. *Case or cannister,* Ch,hee*n*ta gola, gunj gola. *Chain,* Zunjeer wala gola, sankul gola. *See Chain. Double headed or bar,* Doobral gola, *dand*iyara gola, lut,hiya gola. *Grape, See Grape. Round,* Top ke moo*n*h ke burabur gola. *Small,* Bundooq kee golee.

To shot the guns, Topo*n* me*n* gola b,hurna.

Shot lockers, Gole ka koondee, gole ka t,hala.**

Shrouds, Lubran. *Bentinck,* Kras lubran. *Bumkin, Boomkin* lubran, *boomkin* buras. *Bow sprit,* Subdura lubran. *Futtock or foothook, See Futtock. Top mast,* Gavee lubran. *Top gallant,* Suburlubran.

* The lascars make more use of *ka* or *ke*, yet either of the three would be perfectly understood.

** *Gole ka t,hala* is generally used for holding grape shot.

To shut in, Ank,h ke wulut hona.

Sick birth, Azaree ka t,hikana.

Sick list, Be-aramee ka nam ka kaghuz, azaree ke nam ka furd.

Side, Boordoo, bordoo. *Wall sided*, *See Wall.*

Signals, *Seeknel*, *sitnel*, isharu. *Day*, Din ka *seeknel*. *Fog*, Ko,ase kee und,haree ka *seeknel*. *Night*, Rat ka *seeknel*.

To make signals, *Seeknel* kurna, isharu kurna, *seeknel* hukarna, khubur puhoonchana.

Signals of distress, Mooseebut ka *seeknel*.

To make signals of distress, Mooseebut ke *seeknel* hukarna, *oolta* buota hukarna.

To silence a battery, Morche ko markur choop kurana, morche ko marke sir *oot,h*ane nu dena.

Skeet, Ch,hant marne ka doonga.

Skids or skeeds, Dufra, g,husore ke tukhte.

Skiff, Kaghzee muchwa.

To skin up a sail in the bunt, Ser,h ka purdu *tat* kur band,hna.

Sky scrapers, Gubur.

Slab lines, Pulung.

Slack of a line, Alat ka *sulug*, alat ka d,heela.

Slack rigging, D,heela *ringeen*, *ringeen* sub *sulug*.

Slack in stays, P,hirne men ahiste, gos men munda, *as applied to a lascar*, kam men munda.

Slack water, Nurum panee.

To slack, Nurum kurna.

Slings, *Suleeng*, leeng.* *Boat*, Muchwe ka *suleeng*. *Of a buoy*, *Boye* ka arsa. *Of a yard*, Pirmum ka *suleeng*, purwan ka *suleeng*.

Slip, D,huliktee juguh.

To slip a cable, Humar ka ponta ch,hor dena.

Slip knot, Chutput ka giro, churput ka giruh, *suluk* giruh.

Slippering hitch, *Suluk heench*.

Sloop, *Suloop*, suloop.

Slops, Bikroo poshak, bikroo libas.

To slue, Chutur kurna, chatur kurna, guttee kurna.

Smoke sail, G,hoom ser,h, d,hoo,*an* ka ser,h.

Smuggler, Mahsool ka choo*tt*a.

To snack, Raksee dena.

Snatch block, Nuk*t*a kupa, gul ku*t*a kupee.**

Sole of the rudder, Sookan ka chup,d, erab ka tuloo,e.

To sound, Panee mapna.

Soundings, Neeche kee mittee.

In soundings, Proom lugne kee juguh.

Sounding rod, Boombe ka seekh.

South, Duk,hun, junoob, soolee. *East*, Ugin ka ukurub, soo-

* *Leeng* is used by the lascars from G,hog,ha, Surat, &c.

** The first term may be translated, a block with its nose cut, and the second, a block with its throat cut.

lee matlu,e ukurub. *West*, Nuerit, soolee kiblu,e ukurub.

Span, Buras ka mat.

To span in the rigging, Arvil torna.

Spanker, *Drawul*.

Spare, Falto, p,haltoo.

Spars, Faltoo *boom*.

Speaking trumpet, Boongul.

Spear, pump, See Pump.

Spell, Baree, waree, budlee.

So spill, Ser,h bujana.

Spilling lines, Doobral pulung (*also called* jolee.)

Spindle, Seekh, seek,h. *Of capstern*, K,heel, kuwela.

Spirit room, See Room.

Spirketting, Undur ka sinta, undur ka sit.

Splice, the cunt, Buchu *pulas*, panw *pulas*, ch,heen ka *pulas*. *The eye*, Ank,h ka *pulas*. *The long*, Lumba *pulas*. *The short*, Toon ka *pulas*.

To splice, *Pulas* kurna, sand,hna, chapana, chumpana.

Splinters, Gole ka *oor-uele* tookre, gole ka rezu. *Netting*, Gole kee jalee.

Split, Cheer p,har. *On a rock*, Put,hur pur toota.

To be split, Cheer p,har hona.

Spoon drift, Muoje ka ch,hant.

Spray, Mouje ka ler.

Spring, rope, Ara par-ne ka pagur.

To spring a butt, Tukh-te ka sand,ha ch,hoot jana. *A leak*, *See leak*. *The luff*, Gos jana. *A mast.*

Spring tide, Bura juwar, bura kutal.

Sprit, Sail, Subd,hura ser,h. *Sail top sail*, Subd,hura gavee. *Top gallant sail*, Subd,hura subur.

Spunge, Peenchee, soomb,ha.

To spunge a gun, Poochara p,herna, peenchee kurna.

Spun yarn, *Ispiyan*, *Yarn winch*, *Ispiyan* kee chirk,hee.

Spurling line.

Spurs of the beams, Ad,ha *beem*, ad,ha ara.

Squadron, Juhaz ka tolee.

Squ*all*, J,hupe*t*, goonj huwa. *Black*, Budlee ka j,hupe*t*a. *White*, Saf j,hupe*t*a, sook,ha j,hupe*t*a. *Thick*, Bursat ka j,hupeta.

Square, long, Jahom, burabur lumba. *Rigged*, Purwan wala juhaz. *Sail*, Seekee wala ser,h pirmum wala ser,h. *Sterned*, Chuorus duboosa.

Staff, Ch,ho*t*a buota kat,hee,* ch,ho*t*a wuota kat,hee.

Staff, ensign, Bura wuota kat,hee. *Flag*, Oopur ka wuota kat,hee. *Jack*, *Jak* wuota kat,hee.

Stage, for carpenters or caulkers, &c., Purancha. *Floating*, Tirta purancha.

* This word is pronounced also *katee*; see Flag.

Stanchion, Tenchun, k,hoontee.

To stand in shore, Kinare ke nuzdeek jana.

To stand off, Kinare se bahur jana.

To stand by, a sheet, Tueyar ruhna, hat,h me*n* ruk,hna.

To stand on, Woohee mojure me*n* ruhna.

To stand off and on, Heriya marke p,hirna, p,hirta ruhna, ana jana kurna, heriya*n* bariya*n* kurna. *See To tack.*

Standing part of a tackle, &c., Yaree ka mool hat,h.

Standing rigging, See Rigging.

Starboard, Jumuna boordoo, jumunee boordoo, ooja boordoo.

To start, Khalee kurna.

The anchor, Nungur hilana, nungur ulga kurna.

Station bill, Haziree ka kaghuz.

To stave, Soolak kurna.

Star, Tara, sitara.

Star gazer, Titchiya.

To start a butt, Tukhte ka sand,ha k,hoolna.

Stay, Suwa,ee.*

Spring, Pur suwa,ee.

Sail, Ser,h suwa,ee.

Tackles, Suwa,ee yaree.

Steep to, K,hura kinaru, oond,ha.

*Steerage.***

To have steerage way, Sookan manna.

To steer, Sookan pu-

* Often called by Europeans *Savoy!*

** I have not been able to get any term for the above.

kurna, juhaz chulana.

Steersman, Sookanee.*

Stem, Unneeka mook,hra.

To stem a tide, Panee t,hamna, t,hob ruk,hna.

From stem to stern, Unnee se duboose tu,een, unnee se duboose lug.

Stemson.

Step, Dol ka putree, paree, dol ka saree.

To step a boat's mast, Muchwe ka dol k,hura kurna.

Stern, Duboosu, pich,hil. *Chase*, Duboose ka top. *Board*, Oolta manch. *Fast*, Duboose ka pagur. *Frame*, Duboose ke tukhte.

Stern ports, Duboose kee baree, duboose kee bariyan. *Post*, K'hura put,han, koodas. *Sheets*, Muchwe ka peech,hil.

To have stern way, Peech,he hutna, peech,he ana, peech,he melna.

By the stern, Peech,hil boj,ha,ee, peech,he b,haree.

Sternmost (*ships*), Peech,he wale juhaz.

Steward, *Istoor, istor!*

Stiff (*as a ship*), Ser,h t,hobne wala.

Stirrups, Tunnee ka anchka, tunnee ka g,hora.

Stock (*sea*), Beesee, beesee kanta. *Of an*

* Called often by Europeans *Seacunies!*

anchor, See Anchor.

To stock to, Dange men luptee lugana, *istok* lugana.

Stocks, Juhaz ka mundan.

Stock tackle, Dange ka luptee.

Stoppers, Bose.

Stopper (of the anchor), Nungur ka bosu. *Of the cable, or deck,* Tootuk ke bose. *Dog,* Dol ka bosu, k,hun ka bosu. *Of the rigging, Ringeen* ke bose. *Wing, Beem* ke bose.

Stores (naval), Juhazee surinjam, juhazee surumjan.

Store keeper, Bunsar ka sahib, bungsal ka sahib. *Room, Istoor* khanu. *See Room.*

Storm (gale), Toofan, and,hee.

Stowage, K,humal, sumal.

Strait, a, Gala, k,hooch.

Strakes or streakes, Pultee, koostad ke tukhte, seemun ke tukhte. *Garboard,* Mor ka tukhtu, mundan ka tukhtu, mohuree ka tukhtu.

Strand (of a rope), Pan, pam. *Sea beach,* Duriya kant,ha, duriya ka kinaru.

Stranded (as a rope), Ek pan *tootela.* *As a ship,* (Juhaz), kinare pur *tootela.*

To stretch along a brace, Buras, lumba kurna.

To stretch out, Lumba tanna, lumba hulesa tanna.

Stretch (tack), Manch, gos.

Stretcher, T,hant,h ka

tukhtu, t,hat,h marne ka tukhtu.

Stretching, T,hesum t,hes hukarkur, mat,he mat,h hukarkur.

To strike, T,huska k,hana, t,hokur k,hana.* *Lower or let down,* Uriya kurna.

To strip the masts, Dol se *ringeen* nikalna, dol se *ringeen* batil kurna.

String, Mez ke burabur ka tukhtu, oopur tukhtu. *See Chain wales.*

Stroke or sweep of the oars, Anch ka heench.

Strokes man, Lam wala, lam hulesa wala.

Strop, Arsa. *A block strop,* Kupee ka arsa.

Strop iron, Lohe ka arsa.

Studding sail, Dustoor. *Lower,* Neeche dustoor. (*By prefixing the words* gavee, subur, etc. *the top mast, top gallant, etc. are formed.*

Sunken rocks, Doobuo khurabu.

Super-cargo (*an Englishman*) *Turnee, tunnee.*

Super-cargo (*a Moosulman*), Nakhooda.** *A Parsee,* Kiranee, goomashtu.

Supply.

Surf, Ler.

Surge, Muoj, muoju.

* This term is also used ashore as applied to man, horse, &c. stumbling.

** This is compounded of *Na*, which is I think a contraction for *Na,o* a ship, and *khooda* a master.

See Ware.

Surgeon, Daktur, Duktur, hukeem.

Survey, Tulashee, tahkeek, takheet, (*properly* tu*h*qeeq).

Swab, swab, sup, sop. Hand, Ch,hota *swab.*

Swabber, Swab p,hirane wala.

Swab wringers, Swab nichorne wala.

To sway (*to hoist*), Hukarna,* oopur dena. *The top gallant masts,* Subur dol mat,he marna.

Sweep of the tiller, Bukre ka kuman.

Sweeps, Bura hulesa, juhaz ka hulesa.

Sweeping, Lot,haree.

To sweep, Lot,haree *d*alna, billee *d*alna.

Sweepers, J,haroo wala, topus.**

Swell, Duriya ka p,hoolas.

Swifter (*a rope to confine the bars of the capstern,*) Baree ka sat, baree ka ch,hera.

Swifters (*shroud*), Burandul, Burandal, burundu. *For a boat,* Muchwe ka ha*n*s dufra, ha*n*sulee ha*n*s dufra.

To swing, P,hirna, g,hoomna.

Swivel, Jumbooru, zumbooru.

* Perhaps, a corruption from the Portuguese verb *icar*, to sway up, with the addition of *na*, the sign of the Hindoostanee infinitive.

** I cannot find out to what language this word properly belongs; *topus* does not signify a sweeper in the Hindoostanee, but a person of this name generally performs the duty of a sweeper on board most India ships.

Swivel, B,huonr kuree, bumur kuree, b,huonr kulee.

T.

Tacling, putte.

Tack, Moora. *The fore*, Trikut moora. *The main*, Bura moora. *The mizen*, Kilmee moora.

Tack, Manch, gos.

To tack, Heriya marna, heriyan lena.

Tacking, Heriyan markur, heriya lekur.

Tackle, Yaree, *tacklee*. *See Shears*.

Tackle, ground, *See Ground*. *Luff*, Bura luptee. *Tack*, Moore ka luptee.

To top, Kutree kurna.

Top armour, Panjre ka asra. *Block*, Panjre ka kupee. *Chain*, Panjre ka zunjeer. *Cloth*, Panjre ka purdu. *Lantern*, Panjre ka fanoos. *Laying*, Googra, g,hoor g'hoora. *Men*, Panjre wale. *Mast*, Gavee dol. *Gallant mast*, Subur dol. *Rope*, *Tap roos*, *tap ruk*, *tap roop*. *Sails*, Gavee.* *Gallant sails*, Subur. *Gallant studding sails*, Subur dustoor. *Tackle*, *Tap roos* ka yaree.

To top the oars up, Hulese k,hure kurna.

Topping lift, Faltoo muntela ka yaree.

To touch, Bujna.

To touch at, Bundur kurna.

* *Port*. Gaveas.

Touch and go, Lugta jata.

To tow, Pagur band,hna.

To tow over board, Band,h kur panee men *d*alna.

Tow line, Ch,hota *hansel*, virador.* *Rope*, Pagur.

Track of a ship, *See Wake.*

To track, Pagur se tanna, lot,haree tanna, g,hun tanna, luot,-haree marna.

Trade, Suodaguree, bepar, vepar. *Winds*, Muomee huwa, moheemee huwa, muosumee huwa.

Trader, Suodagur, beparee, veparee.

Train of a gun carriage, Garee ka peech,hil. *Of gunpowder*, Baroot d,har, baroot ka runjuk.

Train tackle, Top ke peech,hil kee luptee.

Transoms, Duboose ka ara *beem*, koodas ka *beem*.

Transport, a, Fuoj k,hate ka juhaz.

To transport a ship, Juhaz ko le-jana.

Traveller, a thimble, etc., Satiya *teemlee*.

Travelling back stays, Faltoo furodee, p,hal-too furodee.

Travelling martingale, Chaloo mu*t*un g,hu,ee. **

Tree nails, Tukhte milane kee chabee,

* *Port.* Virador.

** Perhaps this word may be a corruption of martingale.

tukhte lugane ke chimte.

To trend, J,hookna.

Trestle trees, Zumboora.

To trice, Batlee champna, ser,h suptana, supta dena.

Tricing line, Sat, sant.

Trim, T,heek wujun, buraburee.* *Of the sails*, Ser,h kee t,heeka,ee.

To trim the sail, Ser dooroost kurna.

Sharp trimmed, *Buras* chikar.

Trip, K,hep, mat,ha.

Tripping, Anchka. *Line*, Subur purwan ka *gatleen*.

Trough, Muoje ka d,hor, muoje ka d,hap.

Trowsers, Pa-jamu, ijar, izar.

Trucks of a gun carriage, Chak perhe.

Truck of the mast head, Topee ka roda. *Of the parrels*, Luddoo, gotke. *Of the shrouds*, Gole wala luddoo, gol luddoo.

Trumpet, speaking, Boongul, b,hongul, b,hoongul.

Trunnions, Top kee moot, top ka kan.

Truss, Sar, bustar. *Tackle*, Sar kee yaree, bustar kee yaree.

Try sail, Kilmee, kulmee.

Tub, tup, tub, a perfect tub or dull sailer, Juhaz gude ke burabur, put,hur ke burabur,

* I do not think that the above words correspond with *trim*, but I have inserted them, not being able to get better.

Grog, Shurab ka *tup*.
Match, Top ka *tup*.
Top sail haliard, Gavee hunje ka *tup*.
Tuck, Kodas ka m*oor*, k*oo*das ka mor, kilin.
Tumbling home, Moor,h, ch*oo*st, dubun.
Turk's head, Bosu giruh, bosu giro.
Turn of the tide, Tan ka p,her. *Of a rope*, Bolta.*
Turn in the hawse, Umar kee g,huree, umar ka bolta.
To turn in, Sone ko jana, aram kurna.
To turn out, Oo*t*,hkur ana.
To turn in a dead eye, Mutam band,hna, motam band,hna.
To turn over men, Admiyo*n* ko zimme kur dena, somp dena, sipoord kur dena.
To turn the hands up, Admiyon ko oopur bolana.
To turn to windward, Wa,o pur p,hirana.
Twine, Sootlee.
Tye Tue.

V.

Van, Puhila har, puhila qutar.
Vane, Kutwa,ee,** *bend,h, ben*.
Vane, distinguishing, Nisan ka *bend,h*, puhchan ka *ben*. *Dog*, Ma,ee.
Vangs, Turnal, t*oo*rnal.
Veer about, G,hoomnà g,hamna.
To veer and haul, Uriya kur tanna.

* In Italian and Portuguese *volta*, the turn of a rope.
** The lascars from *Kuch,h* use the word *kutwa,ee*.

To veer away the cable, Humar uriya kurna, humar uriya kur dena.

Veering ship, See, To ware.

Vent, Runjuk, kan.

Vessel, Juhaz. *See Ship.*

To unballast, Neerum khalee kurna, neelum khalee kurna, leelam khalee kurna.

To unbend, a sail, cable or stay, K͵hol *d*alna, k͵hol dena, maliya k͵holna. *To take any rope out of a block,* Batil kurna.

o unbit, Habeet se nikalna.

Under current, Neeche ka tan.

Under foot, as said of the anchor, Pet ke neeche.

Under sail, Ser͵h bur͵-ha juhaz chulta.

Under set, Undur ka tan.

To under run, Muchwe me*n* jakur humar dek͵hna.

To under run a tackle, Yaree ka *fal* reenga nikalna.

To unlace, Lasun k͵holna.

To unmoor, Ek nungur pur ruhna.

To unreeve, Batil kurna.

To unrig, Ringeen nikalna.

To unship, Nikalna, bar kurna.

To unsling, Suleeng nikalna.

Volley of small arms, Barurubu.

Volunteer, Jan-baz,

juwan murd. *

Voyage, Sufur. *See Passage.*

Up and down, *Peek.*

Upper deck, Oopur ka tootuk. *Works*, Panee ka oopur juguh.

Upright, Seed,ha.

W.

Wad, Top ka booch.

Waft, Oolta ba,ota. *Literally, a reversed Flag.*

Waist, Beech ka tootuk.

Waist cloths, Jolee d,hampne ka *tirpal*, boordoo ka purdu, jalee ka purdu.

Waisters, Beech ka kam kurne wale.

Wake, Panee ka kut, seer, panee ka wud,h, awuree.**

Wales, Kumurbund.

Wall sided, K,hura boordoo, boordoo deewal ke burabur.

Wall knot, Jolee giro, jolee giruh.

To ware, B,hare p,hirana, damun boordoo p,hirana.

Warp, Pagur, *hansil*. *Of shrouds*, Lubran ka beech. *Woof*, Sootlee.

To warp, Pagur tanna, *hansil* tanna.

Wash.

To wash cloaths, Kupre d,hona, saf kurna.

Wash board, Muchwe ka faltoo *rel*, muchwe ka d,har.

* Sometimes the word *bulumteer* is used; this is not a corruption, but an imitation of the English word, as *bulum* signifies a spear, and *teer* an arrow.

** This last word is used by the Bengal lascars.

Watch, Por, chuokee. *Anchor*, Nungur dek,hne ka por, bundur ka por. *Dog watch*, Ch,hota por.* *Middle watch*, Doosra por, beechila por.

Watch, morning, Goriya por, g,huriya por, g,hooriya por.

To set the watch, Por bantna.

Watcher the first, Puhila por.

Watch glasses, time, G,hureekee sheeshee.

Water, Panee, jul, ab.** *Fresh*, Meet,ha panee. *Salt*, K,hara panee, nona panee. *Line*. Panee ka *marka*. *Loaded*, Boj,ha,ee ka *marka*. *Sail*, Pan dustoor, panee dustoor. *Spout*, Hat,hee soond, *** hat,hee ka panee oot,hula, hat,hee soond ka panee. *Ways*, Purnalu, boornalu. *Logged, ship*, Panee men buet,hguya juhaz.

Watering place, Meet'he panee kee juguh.

Wave, Muoju, muoj.

Way, of a ship, Roos, chal, ruv, churk.

Weather, muosim. *See Wind*.

Weather or weather-gage, wind-ward, Wa,o-pur, ba,opur.

Weather bit, Rook,ha

* The lascars, by way of fun, also use the term *chor por*, (literally, the thief's watch).

** The Arab sailors use the word *ma*.

*** Literally, an elephant's trunk.

bolta. *Boards*, Panee ka asra, ad,hee baree. *Cloth*, Jooliyon ka purdu. *Helm*, Wa,o-pur bukra. *Shore*, Wa,o-pur ka kinaru. *Tide*, Wa,o-pur jane wala tan. *Rolls*, Wa,o-pur ka ara lot. *Beaten*, Toofan ka mara, dook,h ka mara.

To weather, Wa,o-pur chur,hna, ba,o pur jana.

To weigh, Nungur oot,hana, nungur utrung kurna.

To weigh, to raise, oot,hana.

Well, Bumbee kee petee. *Room of a boat*, Gumturee, gamut khanu, bund,hal. *See*, *To spring a Leak.*

Wharf, G,hat, d,huka.*

Wharfinger, D,huke ka piyadu, g,hat ka piyadu.

Wheel of the helm, Sookan ka churkhee.

Welps of the capstern. Duor ka t,happa, duor ka sir, duor t,huk.

West, Mughrub, puch,hum, qiblu,ee *See North and South.*

Whip, Sinjal yaree, gablin.

To whip, Ponta band,hna. *See To point.*

To whip or whip up, Sinjal yaree se hukarna.

Whistle (*boatswain's*), Seetee, *See Call.*

Whoodings, Sal.

* Used by the lascars from Bombay, Surat, G,hog,ha, &c.

Wild roadstead, a, K,hoolasa nungur waree.

Winch, Churkhee.

Wind, Huwa, wa,o ba,o (*a fair wind*) Yahom huwa, jahum huwa, ba moorad huwa. *See Fair.* (*a side wind*), Chuo gosee huwa, char gosee huwa, (*a head wind*), Gosatee huwa, moonh pur huwa.

Wind and water (between), Panee sund,h, panee lub (*a shot between),* Panee lub gola.

To wind a ship or boat, Agil peech,hil g,hoomana.

To wind a call, Seetee bujana.

Wind's eye, Huwa ka g,hur. (*Literally, the wind's house*).

Wind bound, Huwa khurab.

Windlass, Cheena,ee duor, d,heeglee. (*Spanish),* Cheena,ee hubesun.

Wind rode, Huwa ke sam,hue ruk,ha. *Sail,* Puwun ka ser,h, *ven* ser,h.

To windward, Wa,o pur, huwa ka moon,h.

Wingers, Ch,hota peep.

Wings, Bar ka juhaz.

To woold, Kuoree lena, *lasun* lena, chapra lena, bundee kurna.

To work a ship, Juhaz k,herna, Juhaz chulana.

To work (as a ship), Hal huwalee hona.

To work double tides, Doobral kam kurna.

To work up junk, Joong

k,holna.

To work to windward, Heriya markur wa,o pur jana.

Worm (instrument), Ankra, pench. *Eaten*, G,hoon k,ha,ela, g,hoon ka k,hadela.

Worms, etc. (which are so destructive to ship's bottoms), Nona, ood,-hu,ee. (*In the inside*), Deenuk, (*or*) deemuk, g,hoon.

To worm, Raksee dena.

Wreck, K,hok,hra, k,hok,hera, tootela juhaz. *See Cast away*. *Pieces of*, Koch, koonchu.

To wring a mast, Numana, jook,hana.

Y.

Yacht, Suwaree ka muchwa.

Yard, Purwan,* pir-mun. (*Dock yard*), Godee ka bungsal, godee ka bunsar.

Yard arm, Pirmun ka las, purwan ka las.**

Tackle, Las yaree. *Arm and yard arm*, Lasen las, boordoo,*en* boor-doo.

To brace the yards, *Buras* lugna.

To square the yards, Pirmun jahom kurna, purwan yahom kurna.

Yarn, Sun ka ans, sun ka tar, sootlee.

* *Purwan*, I think, is compounded of *Pur* a wing, or feather, and *Wan* a ship, which last word is much used by the lascars from Surat, (properly Soorut) G,hog,ha, Sind,h, Kuch,h, and Goojurat, &c., so that *Purwan*, the yards of the ship, might also be translated the wings upon which the ship flies.

** In Portuguese *Laiz* is the term for a yard arm.

Yaw, Uwaree.

To yaw (a ship), Uwaree dena.

Yeoman, Kusub, mal bhundaree.

Yoke, Sookan kee patlee, sookan kee mankree.

Younker, Juwan.

Z.

Zenith, Kupal ke oopur.

WORDS OF COMMAND

AND

SEA PHRASES.

A.

Abaft the main mast, Bure dol ke peech,-hil.

Aboard the main tack, Boordoo bura moora.

About ship! Tueyar juguh juguh.

A fair wind, Jahom huwa, seed,ha ba,o. *See Favourable.*

All hands to quaters hoay! Sub admee upnee upnee juguh nor top pur jakur tueyar ruho.

All hands reef top sails hoay! Ure! Sub admee *reef* band,hne ko oopur a,o.

All hands splice the main brace hoay! Soono! Sub admee kilmee damun tan; kilmee damun tanne ke waste sub admee a,o.

All hands up anchor hoay! Sub admee b,hur *baree,* (*or*) *d*al duor men humar b,hur *baree.*

All in the wind, Juhaz ke ser,h sub bujte huen.

All's well! Sub uch,ha hue, *alzber.*

Are you ready? Tueyar hue?

Avast! Hoho.

Avast bracing up! Hoho bus mut lugo *buras.*

Avast heaving! Bus nor mut hubeso! ho pal! ho hoodar!

B.

Back all the sails! Baksee agil peech,hil.

Back the main top sail, *Baksee* bura gavee.

Bear a hand! Juldee a,o; juldee kuro.

Bear away, Damun ja.

Before the beam (or either side), Dawa (ya jumuna) *ket* burabur. *See Starboard and Larboard.*

Belay! Band,h.

Brace about the yards! Lug *buras;* purwan p,hira,o.

Brace about the after yards! P,hira,o peech,hil.

Brace round the head yards! P,hira,o agil.

Brace up and haul aft! Lug *buras* tan damun.

Brace the yards sharp up! Lug *buras* chikar.

Bring to the messenger! *Masindur* ka ponta la,o duor men b,huro, (*or*) *dal* duor men *masindur.*

C.

Call the watch! Poree boola,o.

Call the watch hoay! Poree oopur a,o.

Cant the sprit sail yard! Lug b,hare ka subdura *buras.*

Clap on the stoppers before the bits! Habeet ke agil bose band,h.

Clap on the cat fall! *Ket fal* pukur lug;

ket fal lumba kur.

Clap the nippers well on! Uch,hee turuh *neepur* band,h.

Clashees! haul taught the main trusses! Khulasee! bura sar *tat* kuro.

Clear away! Saf kur, mila,o.

Clear away the jib! Saf kur jeeb.

Clew up the main sail, *Istingee* bura ser,h.

Come no near! Ziru damun ja.

Does the ship answer her helm or not? Juhaz sookan ko manta hue ki nuheen?

Down all chests! Tumam petee neeche ruk,ho; sub sundooq neeche do.

Down all hammocks! Tumam j,holee neeche ruk,ho; sub j,hoolee neeche do.

Down fore sail! Mel tirkut.

Down jib and stay sail! Tan neeche *jeeb* suwa,ee.

E.

Ease the ship! (*or helm*), Gos damun, ziru gos damun ja.

F.

Fill the top sails! B,hur gavee.

Fill the main top sail! B,hur bura gavee.

Flatten in the head sheets! Buja,o agil, (*or*) buja,o tirkut suwa,ee damun.

Flat in forward! Haleloo agil.

Fire! Ch,horo, maro, dagho. *See, To fire.*

Fore sheet, fore top bowline jib and stay

sail let go! Ch,hor de tirkut damun tirkut gavee *boolin jeeb* suwa,ee damun.

The fore top sail is a back, Tirkut gavee *baksee* hue.

From clue to earing, Sir se panw lug; neeche se oopur tuluk.

Furl the main top gallant sail! Lupet le bura subur; band,h le bura subur.

G.

Get your oars to pass! Hulesa tueyar ruk,ho.

Get the buoy up! Boya oopur la,o tueyar ruk,ho.

Give her a good coat of tar! Oos men uch,hee turuh ek t,hur *tar* luga,o.

Give way together! Tan zor burabur.

Give way! Tan zor.

Go aloft and reef top sails! Oopur ja,o gavee *reef* band,hne ko.

Go to dinner! K,hane ko ja,o; k,hana k,ha,o ja,o k,hana k,ha,o.

H.

Hand over hand! Le chul hathon hat,h; le chul girgir; lug girgir.

Hard a lee! Gos a,o, b,hare ruk,h.

Hard a port! Dawe boordoo chikar.

Hard a starboard! Jumunee boordoo chikar.

Hard a weather! Damun ja, gos ruk,h.

Haul aft the jib sheet! *Jeeb* damun tan chikar.

Haul a board the fore tack! Tan neeche

tirkut moora.

Haul forward! Tan agil.

Haul fore and aft! Tan agil peechˌhil, lag *buras* tan damun.

Haul the main top bowline! Tan agil bura gavee *boolin.*

Haul aft! Tan peechˌhil; peechˌhil tan.

Haul home the starboard main top gallant sheet! Yumuna bura subur damun tan chikar.

Haul aft the fore sheet! Tan tirkut damun.

Haul in the larboard main brace! Dawa bura *buras* lug.

Haul in the weather braces! Lug baˌopur gavee *buras* subur *buras.*

Haul aft the head sheets! Tan tirkut damun.

Haul away the cat! Lug *ket.*

Haul together! Lug sub burabur.

Haul down the jib and stow it! Tan neeche *jeeb* bandˌho.

Haul main sail haul! Pˌhiraˌo bura serˌh; pˌhiraˌo peechˌhil.

Haul of all! Pˌhiraˌo agil.

Haul the after bowlines! Kˌhuraˌo peechˌhil ka *boolin,* tan peechˌhil *boolin.*

Haul the head bowlines! Kˌhuraˌo agil *boolin,* tan agil *boolin.*

He is aloft or on the mast, Wooh dol ke oopur hue.

Heave! Hubes.

Heave all aback! *Bak-*

see agil peech,hil.

Heave away! Hubes.

Heave round cheerly! Juldee hubes.

Heave taught! Hubes chikar.

Heave the lead! Proom dal.*

Heave the log! Tup dal.

Heave to! Baksee gavee, gavee *baksee* kuro.

Heave in the cable! Hubes humar.

Heave in jib and stay sails, or down jib and stay sails! Tan neeche *jeeb* suwa'ee.

Heave out the stay sails! Saf kuro suwa,ee.

Heave and rally! Hubes mera bap, *(or* b,ha,ee) khalee nungur. *Sometimes a little abuse is necessary: as for instance,* hubes sala! buhan *properly* buhin) chod hubes! (*or*) hubes huramzadu! *and when a little of the anchor remains in the water and the ship under weigh much exertion is necessary, then let the officer a head call out,* hubes

* When the lascar receives the order from the captain or officer to heave the long lead line, the moment he heaves it, he calls out *Nakee deed,ho!* This term is used by the lascars from Soorut (*Surat*), G,hog,ha, Sind,h, and Kuch,h. Those from Bombay, Koolabu, and Bengal use the term, *Juhaz sulamut proom hazir!* The Arabs and many lascars of a religious turn, from different parts of India, when heaving the lead, sing out, *Sulloo ulun Nubee,i!* viz. the blessing of God be upon the Prophet (Moohummud). Some lascars use, *oorda beg!*

ek do pal! *Afterwards, when the anchor is hoisted up, let him sing out,* ho pal pal nikal baree *ket* luga,o b,hur gavee!

Heave and aweigh! Hubes *oot,*ha hue.

Heave and in sight! Hubes danga nuzur ata hue.

Heave and pawl! Hubes *pal.*

Heave taught! Hubes *tat.*

Helms a lee! Gos boordoo.

Hoist away! Hukar.

Heave out the stay sails! Saf kur suwa,ee.

Hoist away the main top sails! Bura gavee hukar; hukar bura gavee.

He has not as yet got his sea legs, Yih admee durya ka chal nuheen paya. *This sentence ought to run as follows, according to Hindoostanee Grammar,* Is admee ne ub tuk durya kee chal nuheen pa,ee.

Hook the cat! Ket luga,o.

Hook the fish! Luga,o *p,hish.*

How many knots is the ship going? Juhaz kitnee giruh chulta.

How many sail do you see to windward? Wa,o pur ketne juhaz huen? ba,o pur ketne juhaz nuzur ate huen?

I.

In top gallant sails!

Istingee subur band,h

Is the anchor aweigh? Nungur utrung hoo,a ki nuheen?

Is the jib sheet hauled aft? Jeeb damun chikar tana hue?

I think that ship is about a cable's length a head of us, Muen sumuj,hta hoon ki wooh juhaz ek suo bees bum humare juhaz ke agil hue.

I was obliged to abandon the ship which we took, Upne pukre hoo,e juhaz ko moöj,-he ch,hor jana pura.

K.

Keep a good look out forward there! Khoob dek,h agil.

Keep a good hold of the land, or keep the shore well aboard! Kinare nuzdeek pukur kur ja,o.

Keep in our wake! Humare kut pukur ke chule a,o; (*or*) humare awuree pukur kur chule a,o.

Keep her full! B,huriya ruk,h; b,hura ruk,h; b,hurke ja,o; b,hur ruk,h.

Keep her close at it! Ek kat buje nuheen buje uesa ja; ek put buje nu buje uesa ja.

L.

Larboard watch hoay! Dawa poree oopür a,o; ugla poree (*or* peech,hila poree) oopur a,o.*

* The first term is a literal translation, but not much used by the lascars, as they in place of it use ugla *first,* and peech,hila *second,* according to circumstances.

Launch ho! Ch,hor de *tap rop.*

Lay in off the yard there! *Las* men se undur a,o.

Lay all flat a back! Sub ser,h *baksee* kuro.

Let go amain! Sub milke ch,hor do.

Let go the fore top sail haulyards! Tirkut gavee hunja ch,hor do.

Let go the top gallant braces! Subur *buras* ch,hor do.

Let go the anchor! Ch,hor do lungur, ch,hor do nungur.

Let go the royal haul-yards! Tubur hunja ch,hor do.

Let go the head sheets! Ch,hor de *jeeb* su-wa,ee damun.

Let go and haul! P,hi-ra,o agil, ch,hor de tan.

Let us know when she is short! Humen khubur do jub *peek* howe.

Let fall and sheet home! Ch,hor de istingee champ damun chikar.

Let fall fore sail! Mel tirkut.

Let go the lee sheet! B,hare damun ch,hor do.

Light along the rope! Lumba kur alat.

Light forward the mes-senger! Tan agil *ma-sindur.*

Look out afore there! P,hune wala khoob dek,ho agil.

Lower away, Uriya, ariyan.

Lower cheerly? Uriya

juldee girgir girgir.

Lower handsomely, Ahiste ahiste uriya kur.

Luff, Gos ja.

Luff round or a lee, Ser,h buja,o. (*Literally, Shake the sails.*)

M.

Madras bears south west of Calcutta, Cheena puttun Kulkutte se soolee kiblu,e ukurub rookh hue.

Main sail haul! P,hira,o bura ser,h; p,hira,o peech,hil.

Main top gallant mast head there! Subur koonde pur!

Main top hoay! Bure panjre pur!

Man the capstern! Tueyar ruk,h duor.

Man the main clue garnets buntlines and leech lines! Pulung batlee seeseedor hat,h men ruk,h; hat,h men ruk,h istingee batlee seeseedor pulung.

Man the top sail sheets! Hat,h men ruk,h gavee damun.

Man the top sail haliards! Hat,h men ruk,h gavee hunja.

N.

No near! Ziru damun ja; buja,o mut. *See, Keep her full.*

Nothing off, Hulek, ulek, uesa ja.

O.

Over haul the larboard main lift! Mila de dawa bura mantela.

P.

Pass a seizing, etc., Musalee ka hat,h lo.

Pass the lead line along! Lumba kur hat,hon hat,h proom ka *len.*

Pay down the rope, Alat neeche de.

Pay out, or away the cable, Umar bahur de ; umar uriya kur ; humar tirka,o.

Port the helm, Dawa ruk,h.

Pull away, pull away! Mar heech mar heech.

Pull together! Tan sub burabur.

Pull right a head! Anee burabur tan.

Pull the starboard oars! Tan jumuna.

Put the helm up! Sookan ba,o pur *oot*,ha,o, sookan wa,o pur ruk,h.

R.

Ready about! or about ship, Tueyar juguh juguh. *Literally, ready! every person at his proper station.*

Raise tacks and sheets! Istingee moora damun.

Right the helm! Sookan seed,ha ruk,h, sookan beech men ruk,h.

Round in the weather braces! Hat,h b,hur wa,o pur *buras.*

Row dry! Hat,h duba tan panee nu oore ; chor hulesa tan panee nu buje.

Rowed-of-all, Helan.

S.

Settle the main top sail haliards! Tirka,o bura gavee hunja.

Set up your back stays! K,hura,o, *or tat* kur, pet furoodee.

She mounts twenty guns, Wooh, yih, juhaz bees top ka hue.

Sheet home the top gallant sails! Champ subur damun chikar.

Shove off! or bear off! Dufruo.

Ship the oars! Hulesa dal.

Shiver the main top sail! Bura gavee baja,o.

Ship the bars! B,hur baree.

She holds her own, Yih juhaz *oos* juhaz burabur chulta hue.

Silence! Choop, (*miscalled chub!*) Choop ruho; kyoon bukte ho? kyoon shor kurte ho?

Slacken the laniard! G,hora nurm kuro; g,hoorla *suluk* kur.

Square the yards! Purwan yahom kur, jahom pirmun.

Stand by your top gallant stay sail haulyards! Subur suwa,ee hunje ko tueyar ruk,-ho; hat,h men ruk,h subur suwa,ee hunja.

Stand by your mizen top gallant haulyards! Kulmee subur hunje ko tueyar ruk,ho; hat,h men ruk,h kulmee subur hunja.

Stand from under! Khuburdar neeche.

Stand by to loose the top sails! Gavee ch,horne ko tueyar ruho.

Starboard mizen top sail brace a pull! Jumana kulmee gavee *buras* lug t,hora.

Starboard watch hoay! Jumana poree oopur a,o. *See Larboard*

Watch.

Steady! Halek; seed,ha ja; uesa ja,o; is *moo*-wafiq chule ja.

Steer the ship steady! S*oo*kan burabur ruk,-ho; kahe koo juhaz burabur nuhee*n* chul-ata huramzadu?

Stick out the cable! Hodee humar t,ho*r*a.

Stow the jib! *Jeeb istab* band,h *jeeb; g,hanset* p,hira,o.

Streach out! *to boat-men*, &c., Mar heech; tan zor.

Strike the bell, G,hu*r*ee mar.

Sway away the top gallant yards! Subur purwan hukaro; hukar subur pur-wan.

Surge the messenger, *Masindur* tirka,o, ariya*n* duor, tirka,o duor.

T

Take a round turn of that rope, *Oos* alat ka bolta le.

That ship's sails are all aback, *Oo*s juhaz ke sub ser,h *baksee* hue*n*.

That ship is beating to windward, Wooh ju-haz huwa ke moo*n*h pur jata hue.

That ship looms large, W*oo*h juhaz j,hanka j,hanka nuzur ata kya jane hue bu*r*a; *d*,h*oo*-n*d*,hla sa nuzur ata wooh juhaz kya jane bu*r*a.

That ship carries a press of sail, Wooh juhaz tesum t,hes hukarke chule jata hue; wooh juhaz mat,ho mat,h hukarke jata.

That ship does not answer her helm, Wooh juhaz upne sookan ko nuheen manta hue.

The anchor comes home, Nungur kusar kurta hue.

The anchor is foul, Nungur men bolta pura hue.

The anchor is a trip, Nungur oot,ha hue; lungur utrung.

The cartridge is home, Tonta chikar hue.

The coast is clear, Durya put muedan hue; muedan khalee hue.

The deck has settled, Tootuk buet,h guya hue.

The land looms high, Kinaru j,hunka* j,hunka dik,hata hue pur ooncha nuzur ata hue.

There is leak abreast of the main hatchway, Bure p,halke boordoo men juhaz gamut kurta hue; bure falke ke samne juhaz gamut kurta hue.

The ship has settled abaft since yesterday, Kul se aj juhaz ka tootuk peech,hil buet,h guya.

The ship heels to port, Juhaz dawe boordoo j,hookta.

There are three ships, Sir, seen in the offing, Sahib, teen juhaz bahur nuzur ate huen.

The tide will slacken, Tan nurum purega; tan nurum hoga.

* This word is pronounced also *j,hanka*. See, *That ship looms large.*

The tide slackens, Tan nurm purta hue; tan nurum hota hue.

The wind heads us a little, Huwa ziru ziru chaturta chaturta agil ata hue; huwa g,hoomta g,hoomta agil ata hue.

The wind is right aft, Huwa moo,wafiq; huwa seed,ha hue; huwa jahom hue.

This is some of your handy work, Yih toomhara hat,h ka buna hoo,a, yih tere hat,h ka kam hue.

This sail does not draw well, Yih ser,h huwa khoob nuheen pukurta.

This ship sails best upon an even keel, Yih juhaz seed,ha put,han hokur bihtur se bihtur chulta hue; yih juhaz seed,ha erab hoke bihtur se bihtur chulta hue.

This ship lies very much over (by the force of the wind), Yih juhaz huwa ke zor se kurwut buhoot hota hue; yih juhaz huwa ke zor se buhoot j,hookta hue.

This ship has a list a starboard, Yih juhaz jumune boordoo j,hooka hue; yih juhaz ke yumune boordoo numun hue.

This ship is very leaky, Yih juhaz buhoot gamtee hue; yih juhaz buhoot gamut kurta.

This stick will never answer to make a main top gallant mast,

Bura subut dol is lukree se nuheen bunega.

Together! Sub milke.

Top sail brace haul in! Gavee *buras* lug.

Top the main yard to port! Dawe turuf kutree kur jumuna mantela champ.

Thus, very well, thus! Gos gos.

V.

Very well thus! Uch,ha gos bus.

U.

Unbit the cable! Nikal humar *habeet* men se.

Under the lee of the land, Kinare ke asre men.

Unship the bars! Nikal baree.

Unship your oars! Nikal hulesa.

Up all hands hoay! Sub admee oopur a,o.

Up courses! Tirkut bura ser,h kulmee mar.

Up main sail! Istingee bura ser,h.

Up with the helm! Sookan ba,o pur ruk,h.

W.

Watch! Ch,hor diya.

We settled the land, Hum ne kinaru ch,hota kiya.

We shall fetch to windward of the light house this tack, Is heriye men qundeel ke wa,opur ja,enge.

We shall make a good stretch this time, Yih manch hum lumba ja,enge; is gos men lumba gos ja,enge.

We were standing in shore when we discovered the enemy

stretching to the southward, Jub hum ser,h k,hootakur kinare jate t,he tub dooshmunon ke juhaz ko dek,ka ki t,hesum t,hes hukar kür duk,hun ke turuf jata t,ha.

We saw a ship abreast of Sagur, Hum ne ek juhaz ko dek,ka gunga Sagur ke sam,hne.

What depth of water is there? Ketna panee oonda hue? Ketna panee guehra hue?

What ship do you belong to? Kis juhaz ka admee ho? Kuo wan non manoos ch,he? Kon wan non manoos? *

Where are you bound to? Toom kuhan jane wale? Kid,hur jate ho? Kuhan ja,oge?

The wind is right aft, Peech,he ka seed,ha huwa hue, Peech,he ka huwa aya.

Who is your messmate? Toomhara veeseewala kuon hue?

* The two last sentences are only used by lascars from K,hog,ha, Sind,h, and Kuch,h.

THE END.